Sue Ward

A-Z of Meetings

London and Sydney

Sue Ward is a freelance journalist, researcher and lecturer. She has worked for the TUC and the GMBATU. Her previous books include **Pensions: A Workers' Handbook ; Social Security at Work** and **Organising Things**, all published by Pluto. Sue Ward has been a member of the Labour Party since 1969 and lives in London.

First published in 1985 by Pluto Press Limited,
The Works, 105a Torriano Avenue, London NW5 2RX
and Pluto Press Australia Limited, PO Box 199, Leichhardt,
New South Wales 2040, Australia

7 6 5 4 3 2 1

89 88 87 86 85

Set by *Sunrise Setting*, Torquay, Devon.
Printed in Great Britain by Guernsey Press Co. Limited,
Guernsey, C.I.

British Library Cataloguing in Publication Data

Ward, Sue
A–Z of meetings.
1. Meetings 2. Parliamentary practice
I. Title
658.4'563 A56

ISBN 0 7453 0103 7

Contents

Acknowledgements

The chief acknowledgement must go to the Labour Party, the TUC, several trade unions, and numerous women's groups and community groups for the years of experience with them of meetings good, bad and indifferent. A large number of people helped me with advice and comments, and I'm grateful to all of them.

They include Doug Gowan, Mike Cunningham, Fran Bennett, Ken Jones, Myles White, Pat and Barbara Roche and Hilary Rose; also Paul Crane at Pluto. Ailsa Mosbacher at LVSC helped me find resources and examples. I have been boring all my friends for a year about the book, so thanks to them, and I have experimented with some of my ideas on a TUC Education Methods course and a Putney Resource Centre course, so thanks also to the students there.

The Further Reading on p. 210 gives details of all the books I have used, and I'm grateful for the assistance I have had from them, even if I did not agree with all their ideas! All the mistakes, of course, are my own.

Introduction

This book is aimed at people who go to meetings and especially people who are active in trade unions, political groups (especially the Labour Party), action and campaigning groups, community groups and women's groups, as well as all the other organizations in Britain that make up what is loosely defined as the left. Once you get involved with such groups, you can find yourself spending a great deal of time at meetings, ranging from the large annual conference of a trade union to the small branch meeting of a dozen or so members of the Labour Party.

Some of these meetings have a formal set of rules and procedures. These are operated with skill by those 'in the know' but can confuse others and make them feel alienated and unwanted. The first aim of this book, therefore, is to explain the formal rules and procedures, so that you can find out what is going on.

If, armed with this framework of knowledge, you persevere with the meetings, effectively put across your point of view and demonstrate that you are keen and active, sooner or later you'll probably find yourself elected to a position where you will have to take some part in running the meetings yourself. You could, of course, simply take over the procedures that have been in operation for years and ignore the fact that when you first came into the group you found them hard going and boring; but I hope you won't. The second aim of this book is to look at 'good practice' for those involved in running meetings of groups bound by formal rules and procedures. A meeting can be run efficiently or inefficiently. It can also be run in a way which is more or less friendly and welcoming. People attending can be encouraged to take part, or discouraged. The meeting can be more or less useful in fulfilling its purpose, say, of planning a campaign, or of educating the group members politically.

You will not always be bound by sets of formal rules, however. Many activists are involved in a quite different sort of meeting, that of the much less formal group. The peace movement and the women's movement, for example, do not use the old framework of procedures, but they manage to operate fairly effectively. Sometimes, however, these meetings can degenerate into chaos, or are taken over by a vocal minority; it is not always easy to see how this happens. The third aim of this book is to look at these alternative ways of working and to see what is needed in order to make the group work more effectively. Some aspects of this alternative approach can be imported – perhaps the word should be smuggled – into a more formal setting. Others will only work if people are heavily committed to a different way of running things. Rather than there being two opposing methods, though, the message of this book is that there is a continuous line from the most formal to the least formal. It is for the particular organization to decide where along the line they are, at any one time, and in which direction they want to move.

The book, then, is inended for two types of person. First, the ordinary member of a group, perhaps someone who has just joined, or just become active, who wants to know what is going on; second, the person (perhaps the ordinary member a few months later) who has agreed to take on a particular role in the organization and wants to know how to carry it out. It is not my intention to lay down hard and fast rules; we've had enough of those in the past. The purpose is more to suggest ideas and possibilities. The book is therefore divided into sections on

- The framework of rules – constitutions and standing orders;
- what happens at a meeting;
- what happens at a conference.

In the main sections we look at what the formal procedures are, the way in which they are operated in practice, as well as alternative possibilities. Then there is a section on the law, which outlines the legal position and makes it clear exactly where this puts limits on what you can do. Finally, there are two appendices on 'meetingspeak' and 'etiquette', which are intended as fairly light-hearted summaries of some of what has gone before.

How to use this book

This book does not have to be read from cover to cover; you can dip in and out of it for the information you need. If you are looking at the question of how meetings are run, the headings in the different chapters will give you an idea of what is covered. If you want to check a particular point, look it up in the index. There are a number of checklists and summaries scattered throughout to help you grasp the major points. If you are short of time, you can just consult these lists on their own. They may jog your memory or imagination.

If you are trying to find out, for instance, how to run a formal branch meeting, look also at the sections on alternative ideas. Some of these might be feasible for your group. However, you will need to persuade other people. You could try using some of the methods suggested in this book, for example, organizing people into small groups to discuss what is wrong with meetings at the moment, or preparing a checklist for people to fill in as the trigger for a discussion. Some of you may not agree with all the suggestions you will find here, but hopefully you can use them as a starting point to develop your own ideas.

1. Why do we have meetings?

We don't simply have meetings for their own sake, although sometimes it may feel like that. Some of the reasons for holding meetings are to work ideas out; to organize things that have to be done; to tell people about things that have been done; to try to persuade people who don't share our views; or, most often, a mixture of these.

At the same time, people go to meetings for various reasons. These may be to get things done; to persuade other people to do things; or to find out what's being done. Above all, the purpose of meetings is to discuss, and take decisions, *collectively*, as a group.

To keep things going with more than four or five people at a time participating, you need some sort of structure. If you're all strongly interested in the same thing, and the issues are fairly simple, it may not need to be a very tight one. If the issues are complicated, or there is a considerable amount of sorting out to do, the structure may have to be more rigid. But what are the very minimum requirements?

- You need a way of telling people your meeting is taking place. This could be done over the phone, or by calling round at each other's houses, or by letter. But somehow people have got to know exactly when and where the meeting is if it is to take place at all. They also need to know what's being discussed, so they can decide whether it's worth turning up. One or more people must take responsibility for this.
- You also need to ensure that everyone has a chance to participate in the meeting. That is, that while one person is speaking others don't cut in and interrupt what that person is trying to say, or make it impossible for others to hear what's going on. Similarly, when a person is anxious to say something, s/he must be given the opportunity and not ignored. The group therefore must make someone responsible for this, for **chairing** the meeting.

■ The members of Ellen's group are having a discussion about their common problem as single parents. They don't want to reach decisions or plan a campaign. So they only need publicity about their meetings and a method of running them.

After a while, however, they decide to go further and run a campaign, write a pamphlet, and possibly draw up a babysitting rota.

Now that their meeting is going to take decisions, it will need:

- a list of things to be decided;
- a note of what's been decided;
- adequate warning to those who are going to be affected;
- knowledge of who's entitled to be there and who turns up, and of who should turn up but doesn't;
- agreement about who's doing what.

If in addition your group is part of a larger one, or is taking complicated or controversial decisions, perhaps about spending large sums of money, you also must be clear exactly **what** has been decided. So people may need to word their proposals very precisely, enabling others then to suggest changes, and the participants may have to vote on them. In some cases you might want to ask a smaller group to go away and work out the details of something specific, and then come back and tell the rest of you. And you may have to make sure you know what's happening at other groups to whom you send representatives, and that those representatives are doing what you want.

Finally, if you turn into an organization that holds property, or pays staff, you must have a structure that ensures it's used for the common good, and one that makes clear where the liability falls if something goes wrong. A bank manager is going to want to know you are a genuine group before s/he lets you open an account; a landlord is going to want to know who s/he can collect the money from, and take to court if you default, before letting you rent rooms.

These are all points covered in the **constitution** and the **standing orders** of groups. Many groups manage with fairly vague ones. Others have very formal legal documents. Chapter 1 looks at the constitutions of formal long-standing groups and Chapter 2 at what you will require if you are setting up a new one. Chapters 3 and 4 treat standing orders in the same way.

1.

Constitutions and rules

Organizations such as union branches, political parties, national campaigning and pressure groups and the management committees of voluntary bodies all act within a framework of rules and methods of carrying out their business. Much of this framework will be written down in a set of 'governing documents'.

The secretary of your organization will have an obligation, under your rules, to let you see the documents, although it will not always be easy to persuade him/her to do so.

A voluntary group, even a well-established one, may possess a variety of documents and it may be difficult to find them all. Sometimes only the secretary has a copy of the up-to-date constitution, and there may not be any 'standing orders' at all.

A trade-union branch, a political party, or a local branch of a national group will probably have a **rule book** issued from the headquarters, laying down the rules you must follow. There may also be a supplement, giving recent amendments. Check always that you are looking at the most up-to-date version.

So the first steps, in trying to find out how your organization is supposed to work, are to:

- find out what documents govern it;
- get hold of copies of each;
- check that they are up to date and complete.

Bear in mind, though, that these written documents provide **only** the framework in which the group operates. They can't tell you how the arrangements work in practice. For example, the TUC's Annual Congress has the power to overturn a decision of the general council, but it's almost unheard of to do so. Groups with identical constitutions can be run in quite different ways. One Labour Party branch may leave its executive committee to get on with all the administration, so that the members as a whole hardly ever discuss the financial situation, while another goes through their report line by line.

Types of organization

If you want to know more about the way your organization is run you will need to find out about the legal arrangements that govern your group. These will vary according to whether the group is an unincorporated association; a company limited by guarantee; a co-operative (which could be an Industrial and Provident Society or a Friendly Society); a company limited by shares; or a trade union.

Most small voluntary groups are unincorporated associations. This means they are set up under a framework of rules and a constitution, but they are not 'legal entities'. The law regards them simply as a collection of individuals. If the group is wound up, all the individuals involved will be liable for any debts. If they wish to hold property of any sort, they need **trustees**, who will be appointed by a **trust deed**. This is explained on p. 3, and there is an example of a trust deed in Appendix 3.

Companies limited by guarantee are legal entities, and can therefore hold property in their own name. They tend to be more organized, longer-lasting groups. They have to be registered and then people buy a share in the company – usually at a nominal price – and are only liable for debts up to that amount if the group is wound up. If your group is a company limited by guarantee, then it will have a **Memorandum and Articles of Association**, often called the 'Mem and Arts', which are the equivalent of any other group's rule book.

Companies are not very democratic organizations (though they can be run that way), but being 'incorporated' as one means that the organization is a legal entity and can therefore sue and be sued in its own name. As explained in Chapter 10, the committee could otherwise be liable as individuals. A company can also hold property, while an organization that is not one must have individual trustees.

Forming a company costs several hundred pounds, and means that copies of the annual accounts must be sent to Companies House in Cardiff. If the organization is a company, the constitution will tell you where its 'registered office' is. This is usually the main office, but it does not have to be. A member, who in this case is a 'shareholder' of the company, has a right to inspect the constitution and the accounts at the registered office.

Co-operatives can be set up either as 'Friendly Societies', which are unincorporated associations, or as Industrial and Provident Societies, which are not. In both cases, they have to register with the Registrar of Friendly Societies. These are special types of companies, organized in a way which is intended to make it easier for the workers, and the ordinary members, to participate in their running.

Finally, there are **companies limited by shares** and **trade unions**. An ordinary commercial firm is a company limited by shares; like the other sort of company, it will have a **Memorandum and Articles of Association** which is its basic legal document. Trade unions are governed by their rule book and are regulated by various Acts of Parliament; they have a legal duty to follow democratic procedures and to allow members to see the accounts, for instance. For more information about these, see *Rights at Work*, (see Further Reading on p. 210 for details).

The last two types of organization cannot be charities. The others can, provided the Charity Commissioners accept them. The group's notepaper ought to tell you:

- if they are a charity or not; if they are, it will say 'Charity Registration number . . .';
- if they are a company; or
- if they are a co-operative (and if so which type).

Most constitutions start with the name of the organization, for instance, 'The Association shall be called the Gateway Community Centre Association.' Look at this carefully, because it will tell you quite a lot about the group. If it is a trade union, this clause will say so. If the name has 'Limited' at the end, this means it has been set up as a company (there are some companies without this in their names, but they are rare).

Chapter 10 deals with the law as it affects different types of organization. The booklist on p. 210 also provides details of a number of publications which explain the advantages and disadvantages of these different types.

Trustees

Unincorporated associations (see p. 2) must have **trustees** to be the formal owners of any property. So too, under the Trade Union Acts, do trade unions. In the case of a voluntary body, the trustees are appointed by the management committee and will usually be local worthies, councillors, or similar people.

There may be a separate trust deed, or a clause in the constitution may set out the power the trustees have and what they must do.

The NUPE rules say:

> 1. Six persons shall be appointed as Trustees of the Union, three by the Executive Council and three by the National Conference. They shall not in any way deal with the funds of the Union or part with any document relating thereto except under the direction of the Executive Council, evidenced by a minute to that effect, a copy

of which shall be supplied to the Trustees by the General Secretary, countersigned by the Chairman/woman presiding at an Executive Council meeting.

2. The Trustees shall perform and execute the duties and functions assigned to them by the Executive Council in accordance with the Trade Union Acts. They shall not sell or transfer any property or assets of the Union without the consent and authority of the Executive Council.

An example of a complete trust deed is given in Appendix 3. As you can see, it is a complex legal document and the duties of trustee are arduous. They have to act 'in the best interests' of the beneficiary, which in this case is the organization of which they are trustees. In November 1984 Arthur Scargill and others were removed as trustees of the NUM by a judge who considered they were not acting in the union members' interest, though this is an unusual event.

Trustees have a financial responsibility. For example, if the Utopia Residents failed to pay the rent on their social club, the landlord can sue the trustees for it and they might find themselves liable to pay out of their own pockets.

Some organizations have 'indemnity' clauses in their constitutions which say that the organization will pay any costs incurred if something goes wrong. Before you appoint trustees, it's sensible to check if yours does. It's only fair also to ensure that they know what it could mean before you get them to sign on the dotted line.

The officers and executive committee of an unincorporated association could also be liable, incidentally. You don't get rid of responsibility by appointing trustees. See Chapter 10 on the law for more details on this.

If the group is in debt when it is wound up, the trustees are likely to be liable, unless the organization is a limited company.

Understanding the small print

Having discovered what sort of organization you are, you will know what documents you are looking for. These are:

- the constitution and rules – these may be two separate documents, or else amalgamated into one rule book;
- standing orders;
- perhaps for an 'unincorporated association' a trust deed;
- for an 'incorporated association', a Memorandum and Articles of Association.

The next thing is to work through the various clauses. If you have managed to get hold of the documents, keep them in front of you while reading this chapter, and look up the various items as you come to them. On p. 33 there is a checklist of points for you to refer to.

The constitution and rules can be arranged in any number of different ways, so even if you are looking for just one point, it's wise to check through everything in case another clause adds to, or limits, the previous arrangements.

In particular, check if there are any 'schedules' at the end. These are extra sections added to deal with special subjects, for instance, the powers of the executive committee, or how they run the meetings.

The examples that are used in the rest of this chapter are taken from the constitutions of several different organizations. All of them have their faults, so don't take any of them as a model. The Further Reading on p. 210 suggests places where you can find model constitutions for different types of group.

Many constitutions are very poorly drawn up, or have been made confusing by a series of changes (usually called 'amendments') over the years; these can cause considerable problems for organizations trying to use them. You might find, having searched all the way through your constitution, that it lacks an important section, for instance, one telling you how to end someone's membership.

You will find that some words are given a special meaning in the constitution. This will be laid down either in a special 'Definitions' clause, somewhere at the beginning or, alternatively, the first time the word is used. It will say something like 'hereinafter called the . . .' Here is an example of this:

> The Name of the Association shall be the 'Women and Under 5s Project' (hereinafter referred to as The Project)

Check this, as it may make something clear which is not otherwise.

Most constitutions are written in fairly legal language, which means long words and sentences, often with very few commas.

One Community Association's constitution says:

> The Objects of the Centre shall be (a) the relief of poverty and provision of education by the charitable means of providing equipping furnishing endowing managing assisting and maintaining a community centre for the benefit of persons residing in the area

Lawyers say they do this because, in English grammar, where you put the comma can change the meaning, and so to play safe they tend to leave them out altogether. It can make it difficult to find your way through the sentences, but persevere – you need to know.

The following sections go through the various clauses in constitutions.

Objects

The first major clause or so will set out the aims for which the group was set up. Here is an example of the 'aims and objectives' clause (sometimes simply called the 'objects') for one voluntary group:

> The objects of the Project shall be to promote maintain and advance the education and welfare of children in the Boroughs of Hometown and Awaytown, particularly by the provision of facilities for children's play recreation and pre-school education in which parents can participate where appropriate.

Look in your trade-union rule book to find the objects clause there. It may well be very long. The TSSA's, for instance, has 14 clauses.

Legally these clauses are highly important, because they limit what the group can do. Sometimes they may seem to cover everything the group could possibly want to do. This is because, if the group doesn't have a particular power given to it, the governing body would be breaking the law by acting *ultra vires* – beyond its powers – if they behaved as if they did.

This is particularly important if it's a question of whether the organization has powers to own land and property and to take on staff. A bank or a solicitor, acting for people from whom an organization wants to buy, will want to check the constitution before lending money or letting you have the deeds. So will people giving grants to groups. TSSA rules say they can 'purchase take in lease or in exchange hire or otherwise acquire . . . any buildings or parts thereof' and 'borrow any money required for the purposes of the Association upon such terms and on such securities as may be determined.' A clause like this allows them to own their buildings and get overdrafts.

The objects clause may also tell you the geographical area the organization covers. In the example above, it was 'the Boroughs of Hometown and Awaytown'. Some sets of rules are very restrictive about the area, especially if they are for a community centre or a tenants' club, so, for example, the Gateway Centre rules say that the objectives are:

> managing assisting and maintaining a community centre for the benefit of persons residing in the area bounded by Hometown Lane on the north side, Anyplace High Road and Anytown Hill on the east side and the railway line running from the Common to the

> Station on the south and west sides (hereinafter referred to as 'the Residents').

However, this leaves the position more open than you might think at first, because it doesn't say that only people living in that area can use the centre. The group have decided that it is to the 'benefit' of the people who live in that area if others, from outside that area, use the pensioners' lunch club, because otherwise it won't have enough clients to keep going.

Often, to avoid being restricted, there is a subclause which says that you can do anything that will advance your objects, and this is a catch-all that leaves you fairly free to do what you want.

Membership

The next clause will define who can belong to the organization. The Gateway Centre says:

> (a) Full membership of the Centre shall be open to residents over the age of 18 years;
> (b) A register of full members (hereinafter referred to as 'registered members') shall be maintained in a form to be decided by the Management Committee, but this register must clearly show the names and addresses of such members and date of registration;
> (c) Registered members shall be entitled to attend all general meetings of the Centre and to vote thereat;
> (d) Associate membership without the power to vote at meetings shall be open to residents under the age of 18 years.

If the organization is a company, becoming a member will usually involve buying a share in it. These tend to be priced at £1, so as not to discourage anyone. This is a one-off payment when you first join. There will be a separate membership subscription and you'll probably find the details of that in another clause.

There could be special qualifications; for instance, NALGO only allows people who work in the public sector to become members, and many professional bodies say you must have passed certain exams before you can join. Political groups, such as the Labour Party, often say you must 'subscribe to' – that is, agree with – the aims and objects of the organization before you can join.

Many groups have separate categories of **associate, affiliate,** or **honorary** members, who usually have fewer rights than full members. They may not be able to vote or become committee members.

■ The Resource Project allows people who live and work in the borough, or people who are nominated as the representatives of other local organizations to be full members; but political parties, and people who don't qualify as full members, can still be **associates**. They are entitled to attend general meetings, and to speak, but they must not vote, and must not be counted in the 'quorum' (see p. 22), nor can they be chairperson or sit on the committee.

Affiliate membership can mean two different things. It can be just another word for associate membership. More often, though, groups **affiliate** either to their central or area organization, or to others with which they have links or sympathies. So an area CND committee might have all the local CND committees affiliate, and the local Labour Party might also affiliate, in order to demonstrate their support for CND. The rights of affiliates should be spelt out in the constitution.

Honorary members are usually important people who, in the group's view, will be helpful in some way. A group might ask its local MP to be an honorary member. They are not usually asked to pay a subscription, but nor are they allowed to vote or be on the committee. They are there because it is an **honour**; they're not expected to be active in the group itself, but it is hoped that they will speak up for them when necessary.

The right to membership

In the Gateway example above, if you qualify by living in the area, you have a right to become a member, and no one has the power to keep you out. In other instances, though, the rules lay down a procedure that has to be followed before you can become a member. So the National Union of Public Employees (NUPE) says you must be 'proposed and seconded by members of the branch and adopted by a majority of the members present'. A voluntary group might leave it up to the management committee (see p. 11) to decide whom to let in.

If the constitution allows people to be kept out, it probably also lays down a way of appealing against this. It may be tucked away in a different clause further on. Without this right of appeal, a court would probably say the constitution did not uphold 'natural justice' and therefore the decisions you took were not legally valid. (See Chapter 10 for a fuller explanation of the law.) Usually, this clause will say that you can appeal from the executive to a special appeals committee or to your annual conference, or to a general meeting of the whole membership.

It will be seen, therefore, that a member of the National Front could not be stopped from becoming a member of the Gateway Centre. S/he could, however, be banned from NUPE and would have to appeal to their special appeals committee to be let in.

Ending membership

Many, but not all, constitutions also say how you stop being a member. If there is no rule about it, then once you've joined you can remain a member for life, even if you never pay a subscription.

- The Resource Project says that you stop being a member if you resign, if you stop living or working in the borough, or representing another local organization, if you don't pay your subscription.

  It also says, though, that you can be expelled, if 'a resolution of which notice has been duly given is passed at a General Meeting of the Project by not less than two-thirds of the votes of the members present and voting that the membership of the member is terminated'.

Probably a court would say that the threatened member must be told that the issue is coming up and given the right to put his or her side of the case. The organization would be ordered either to re-admit the person or to go through the process again properly, if the expelled member took legal action.

There are special legal provisions that apply to **trade unions** if being excluded or expelled results in a person losing a job, or being unable to take one up, because there is a closed shop. You have the right to apply to an industrial tribunal within three months and they will then decide whether the union acted reasonably and honestly. If the tribunal decides that the complaint is justified, it can tell the union to accept the application for membership. If this isn't carried out within four weeks, the union can be forced to pay compensation.

Many unions have special rules to cover the case of a member who has been strike-breaking or causing trouble within the union. Often, the powers are very wide indeed, although they may not be much used.

NUPE's rules say:

> If any member of a Branch continually creates a disturbance in the Branch, or circulates misleading or false reports about the Union, or visits other Branches urging them to defy the proper authority of the Union, or attends Branch meetings in a drunken state the Branch to which this member belongs shall have power to suspend

> him or her from attending Branch meetings . . . The Branch Secretary shall report this suspension and the reason to the General Secretary who, following a full enquiry, shall submit the matter to the executive committee, who have power to expel such a member from the Union.

The TUC also has an Independent Review Committee that hears complaints once a person has gone through their own union's appeals procedure. They can recommend, but not compel, a union to let someone in, or allow them back.

People can also sue a union, or a professional organization, if the fact that they are being excluded is making it difficult or impossible for them to earn their living. For more details on this, see *Rights at Work* by Jeremy McMullen, (details in Further Reading on p. 210).

Subscriptions

Another section, which may be separate or may be part of the membership clause, will say what the subscription is, and who is entitled to decide on it. This may be the executive committee, or more usually the annual meeting of members. In organizations which are set up as companies, it's quite common to put in a high figure; the Resource Project says it 'shall not exceed £20', but it then says that the annual meeting has power to fix each year's subscription rate up to that figure. This saves trouble in changing the constitution, but it can look rather off-putting for members who may think they have to pay that figure.

When is your subscription due and when do you get membership rights? This will matter if there is a question of who is allowed to vote at a meeting. The constitution ought to spell out whether you are allowed to act as a full member immediately, or have to wait a specific number of days.

■ The Gateway Centre says that you become, for example, a member simply by registering as one. So a person could turn up with a load of mates a few moments before the annual general meeting starts and register the lot of them, and they can all troop in and vote for chairperson.

The Labour Party, however, says that you are not a member until the branch meeting after the general committee of that constituency has accepted you. So if the same group should turn up to their meeting, they might be allowed to stay and listen, but they couldn't vote until their membership had been approved.

If the subscription is annual, the constitution should say when you have to pay and what happens if you don't. Usually, you can pay any time up to the annual general meeting and still be allowed to vote. Sometimes you are allowed even more time; the Resource Project says you must pay up within one month of the annual general meeting. This would allow you to vote at that meeting, even if you didn't intend to pay any further subs.

Unions normally expect you to pay weekly or monthly. If you're behind by more than a certain amount, you usually lose membership rights. This is called being 'out of benefit' or 'out of compliance'.

- NUPE says you are a 'non-financial member' if you owe more than 13 weeks' contributions, and you forfeit all right to benefits and cannot vote on any business or hold office. After you've paid up, you have to wait six weeks before you have full membership rights restored.

- In the TGWU you have to have been 'in compliance' for a specific length of time before you can stand in any union election. This could mean that if the person who's supposed to collect your sub falls behind on the job, you might find yourself suspended, and so it needs watching if you want to become an officer.

Groups sometimes impose special conditions before you can vote in elections, although you may be a full member for other purposes. The Co-op for instance says you must spend a certain amount in their shops, and the Labour Party says that in order to vote when a new candidate for MP is being selected at their general committee, you must have attended at least two general committee meetings. For anything else, a new member can vote straight away. If there is nothing about this question in the constitution or the standing orders, you can assume that anyone can join and that, as soon as they do, they are qualified to vote.

Management committee

Groups of any size usually have a small committee set up to deal with the day-to-day business, although smaller organizations often do without them. This committee may be called by a number of different names; executive committee or executive council are most common. Some organizations have both a management and executive committee. A group that is a company may have a board of directors instead; and a trade union may have a branch committee. These committees may have different powers in different organizations.

The important committee is the one that has to **manage** the group's affairs and **execute** (carry out) its wishes between the general meetings of members.

This committee may be elected directly from the members, or there may be a two-stage process. The Labour Party, for example, has a general committee in each constituency made up of representatives of all the different branches and unions that belong. This elects the executive committee which is supposed to carry on the day-to-day work of the constituency.

The management or executive committee can spawn subcommittees; perhaps dealing with staff, with finance, or with political action, so that it is difficult for new members to find their way around. It may be a sign that the group is not working very well if every issue seems to be referred to another committee.

Draw yourself a diagram of your organization to make sure you're clear about how it is structured. You may well have to collect the information for this from several different parts of the constitution. So, for instance, a diagram of the Labour Party at constituency level might look like this:

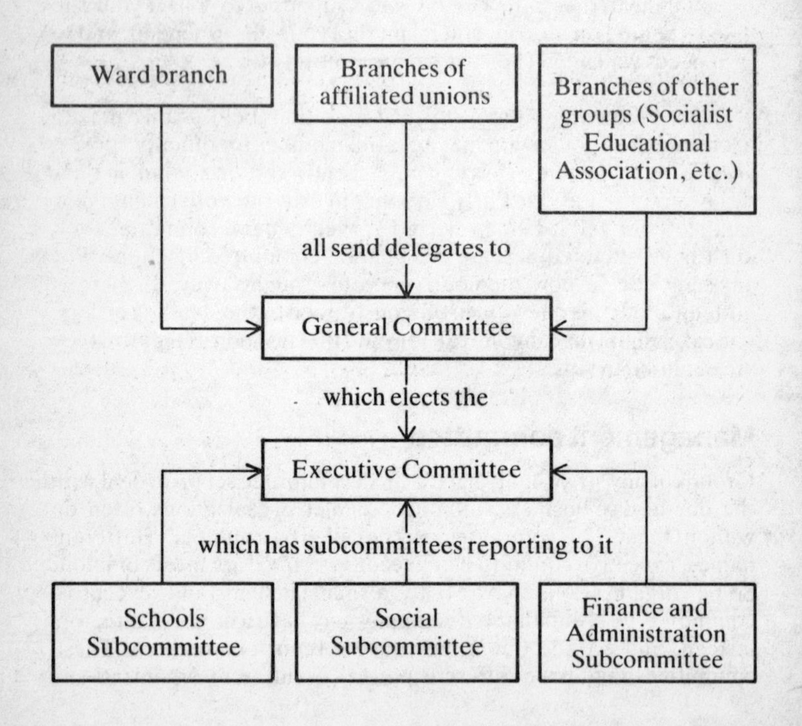

This diagram pins down the essential points: who the committee is; how they get there; what they are allowed to do; who they must tell about what they are doing.

Committee members

The constitution should say how many people are on the committee and how they qualify. A local Labour Party's rules, for example, could say that there are 10 people on the Executive Committee, four of whom must be delegates from ward branches, four from trade unions, one from the Young Socialists and one from the Women's Section.

The Resource Project constitution says:

> Every member of the Project (except a member of the Staff and any Associate) shall be eligible for membership of the Management Committee, provided that no member shall be a member of the Management Committee for more than three consecutive years at a time. The Management Committee shall consist of not more than 25 and not less than 8 Members.

Election or appointment

The constitution will also say who has the power to elect or appoint the committee. Often all the members of the group are entitled to vote. In some cases they will have to turn up at a particular meeting to do so, while in other cases they may do so by post. In some groups they can do both.

If people are to be elected, there will be a clause explaining when this happens, and for how long they will serve.

For the Gateway Community Centre, the rules say:

> Members of the Management Committee shall be elected . . . at the Annual General Meeting of the Centre. They shall hold office until the next following Annual General Meeting . . . and retiring members shall be eligible for re-election.

Next, you will need to understand the mechanics of the election. How can people ensure their names are put forward? Usually, they will need to be **nominated**. That is, someone else will have to say they would like that person to be elected. On pp. 129–133 you will find an explanation of how this works in practice. The constitution will tell you what the arrangements are and how many days in advance you have to send in the nomination.

The Gateway constitution says:

> Nomination forms for election to the Management Committee

> and for the election of Chairperson, Secretary and Treasurer for the next ensuing year shall be sent by the Secretary to all registered members with the notice of the Annual General Meeting.
>
> Nomination forms shall clearly state that the completed forms must be returned to the Secretary not later than ten days prior to the Annual General Meeting and completed forms must clearly show the names in full and the addresses of the nominee and two proposers, who shall be registered members, and shall also be signed by all three.

What if no one is put forward in advance? This can often happen in voluntary groups, where a certain amount of arm-twisting has to go on to get the jobs filled, and often this is allowed for in the rules.

The Gateway constitution says:

> In the event of no nomination for the office of Secretary being received in writing prior to the commencement of the meeting, nominations may be taken from the floor, subject to the nominee being present and assenting, and to his nomination being proposed and seconded. In the event of a Chairperson or Secretary or Treasurer not being so elected, the vacancy shall be filled by election at the first meeting of the Management Committee.

A union, or a larger national group, probably would not have this rule.

Ballots

Once people know who has been nominated for the committee, the next consideration is how to vote for them. Usually you will be told before the actual meeting who the candidates are, so you have time to make up your mind.

So the Gateway constitution says:

> In the event of the number of nominations exceeding the number required, a vote will be taken by ballot at the meeting. The Secretary shall send to registered members the names of persons nominated so as to reach them not later than three days before the date of the meeting.

On pp. 129–133 you will find an explanation of how a ballot works, as well as the different forms of voting.

Proxy voting

Some groups allow you the right to vote not in person, but by giving power to someone else to do it for you. This usually happens where the group is a **company**, and the power for this would be included in the Memorandum and Articles of Association. Here is an example of one, in highly legal language:

> Save as herein expressly provided, no member other than a member duly registered, who shall have paid every subscription and other sum (if any) which shall be due and payable to the Association in respect of his membership, shall be entitled to vote on any question either personally or by proxy, or as a proxy for another member, at any General Meeting.
>
> Votes may be given on a poll either personally or by proxy. On a show of hands a member present only by proxy shall have no vote, but a proxy for a corporation may vote on a show of hands. A corporation may vote by its duly authorized representative appointed as provided by section 139 of the Act. A proxy need not be a member.
>
> The Instrument appointing a proxy shall be in writing under the hand of the appointor or his attorney duly authorized in writing, or if such appointor is a corporation under its common seal, if any, and, if none, then under the hand of some officer duly authorized in that behalf.

The rules may lay down exactly what sort of 'instrument', that is, a form, must be filled in. This is a safeguard against someone turning up with a dirty bit of paper and claiming to hold someone's proxy.

The example below is taken from a housing association's rules.

> I, ____
>
> of ____
>
> In the County of ____________________, being a Member of the Anytown Housing Association, Limited, hereby appoint
>
> Mr/Ms ____
>
> of ______________________________ as my proxy to vote for me on my behalf at the Annual General Meeting of the Association to be held on the 19th December, 1985.
>
> AS WITNESS my hand this ________ day of __________ 198__
>
> Signature: ____

Special nominations or co-options

A group that gets some of its funds from the local council may have to include on its committee some people nominated by the council to keep an eye on them. Such people would be selected by a separate procedure. The Gateway rules say:

> In the case of the Council, the names of members appointed by the Council shall be notified to the Secretary normally within seven days of the Annual Meeting of the Council, and if such notification is too late for it to be submitted to the Annual General Meeting of the Centre, then such appointments shall be submitted to the next following meeting of the Management Committee.

A committee may also have **co-opted** members. These are people who are chosen by the elected committee to join them, after the election has taken place. In some cases these may be the people who lost the election, if the committee is favourable towards them. The idea of co-optees is that they have something special to offer. It could be people who are important locally, like a beat police officer or a community worker. It could be someone to balance the committee better, if, for example, they needed to have more women or black people. Again, it could be a representative of a group you wanted to build better contacts with. So the Child Poverty Action Group sometimes co-opts a member of the Low Pay Unit on to its committee, because the two organizations work closely together and need to know what each other is doing. Or a co-optee could instead be someone who has a particular skill, who is asked to come along to meetings when needed, but not otherwise. So you might invite someone who knows a bit about fund-raising for two or three meetings while you were deciding how to raise some money.

Co-opted members may not be treated as full members in every way. Often, for instance, they do not have power to vote. If they do have full powers, the constitution usually limits their numbers so that they can't swamp the rest of the committee.

Generally a committee selects those it wants to co-opt at the first meeting after its AGM (see Chapter 6). If you want to get someone appointed, take along full details about them and check in advance that that person is willing to stand.

Ex officio members

Finally, the committee may have some members who are there 'ex officio', that is, because they do a particular job. The chair or president of a group is usually automatically a member of the executive committee and also of any subcommittees, and so s/he does not need to be elected to these committees in the same way as other people do.

Casual vacancies

The constitution ought also to say how you fill a vacancy if someone dies or resigns during the year between elections. This is called a 'casual vacancy'. It can involve another election, or the committee may itself appoint someone, or the person who got the top votes among the unsuccessful candidates may fill the place.

Absentees

What if someone does not come to committee meetings? Usually, the constitution says that if you miss a certain number you stop being a committee member. Sometimes this is automatic and in other cases it is up to the committee to decide what to do. So for instance the Gateway rules say:

> If a member of the Management Committee fails to attend three or more consecutive meetings the fact shall be reported to the next following meeting when the Committee may declare that such member shall no longer be a member of the Committee.

Since it says 'may', the committee has some leeway. If they know that person has a lot of domestic problems, they could leave things a while longer. If the clause said 'shall', they would have no power to argue about it.

In the NUPE rules for their executive council one finds another way of giving the committee power to decide. Here it says that you must have 'sufficient and satisfactory reason', which means that the committee will decide whether to accept your reasons or not.

There may also be special rules about people appointed by bodies like the council who give you grants. They might not be expected to turn up so often.

Powers and duties

The constitution will tell you about the **duties** of the management or executive committee. The Gateway constitution, for instance, says they are to 'provide for the administration, management, and control of the affairs and property of the Centre'. This is very general; their job is spelt out further in a separate 'schedule' at the end of the document, headed, 'Rules of the Management Committee'. Separating the clauses in this way is quite common.

> The Management Committee shall have the right to:
> 1. hire premises, provide equipment, engage staff, and arrange insurance related to these matters;

2. refer matters to a solicitor or authorize trustees in various functions;
3. raise money for the Centre's activities;
4. appoint subcommittees to act on behalf of the Management Committee; and such subcommittees may be given the power to co-opt members provided that such co-opted members do not exceed more than one-quarter of the total membership of the subcommittee;
5. authorize such payments as shall be necessary.
The Management Committee may authorize the Trustees:
a) to enter into contracts and borrow money on the security of the trust property;
b) to raise money for use in furthering the objects of the Centre;
c) to apply any part of the trust property or the income thereof;
in and for the purchase renting or hire of freehold or leasehold premises to be used as part of the trust property;
in and for the equipment maintenance repair insurance and general upkeep of the Centre and any other property which may at any time be vested in the trustees and the payment of staff in connection therewith and the general expenses of managing the same.

The committee is restricted by this clause, and cannot go outside the powers laid down here. If, for instance, subclause 2 did not exist in your committee's rules, the management committee would not be able to appoint any subcommittees. If they did so, they would be acting *ultra vires*, which means outside their powers. For an explanation of what happens then, see pp. 194–5.

This particular example gives full power to the management committee to do everything they wish without referring to a general meeting or to the members in any other way. Other constitutions may say that certain things can only be done 'subject to the consent of the General Meeting' or 'subject to a ballot of the members'. So, for example, the National Union of Seamen must ballot its members before it accepts a pay deal or calls a national strike; the executive council has no powers to do this on its own.

Every management committee will have to report at least once a year to an annual meeting; this is dealt with in Chapter 6.

Subcommittees

If the constitution creates the power to appoint subcommittees, as in the example above, it may leave the management committee to decide what they do and how they operate, or it may provide more detailed instructions.

The Resource Project allows the management committee to appoint any subcommittee they want, but says that they must report back to the main committee and not have independent power. The constitution says:

> The Management Committee may delegate any of its powers to subcommittees consisting of such members of its body or such other persons whether or not members of the Project as it thinks fit, provided that all acts and proceedings of such subcommittees shall be reported back and ratified by the Management Committee as soon as possible.

Look again at the diagram you drew up of your organization's structure. Which groups have independent power, and which have to ask permission?

■ In the Labour Party example on p. 12, the schools subcommittee has the power to appoint school governors on its own. So the executive committee could not tell it to appoint Bill to a school whether it liked it or not. The subcommittee tells the GC every three months what they have been doing, but don't have to wait for their agreement. So the most the executive could do is tell them off for appointing the wrong person and say, 'Don't do it again.'

The finance subcommittee, on the other hand, has much less power; it can only recommend to the executive what it does with its money, not act for itself. The executive can turn down its recommendations, and do something different, any time it wants.

The way the **minutes** and **reports** of different types of committees are treated should vary according to the powers they have; this is dealt with on pp. 52–5.

Officers

The rules will tell you what officers the organization has, what their powers are, and how they get there. The usual officers are chair (see also pp. 54–9), secretary (see also p. 59) and treasurer, but there could also be a vice-chair, assistants to the secretary and treasurer, a social secretary, and others. The rules may be very precise about what exactly they do. They might say, for instance, 'The Chair shall preside at all meetings', and this would mean that if you decided to rotate the job among the different members you'd be unconstitutional. It's unlikely that this would matter very often, but it might if there was a query.

The officers could be elected by the organization as a whole, perhaps in the general meeting through a ballot, at the same time as the management or executive committee is elected; or by the committee itself.

Often there are different procedures for the chair, who may be elected by the whole membership, and the others who are elected simply by the committee, as their jobs are seen as less important.

The length of time that the officers remain in the job is usually laid down; it could be a year, but sometimes it is much longer, at least for the chair. It could, on the other hand, be up to the committee itself to decide.

The Resource Project constitution says that the management committee 'shall have power to determine the period or periods for which [the officers] hold office'. This means that they could rotate the job at every meeting if they want.

Attendance

You might want to go along to a meeting of the management or executive committee to see what it's like. Some organizations say that any member of the group can go along.

One constitution says:

> Individual members shall have the right to attend Council meetings and the EC shall arrange for the election of a voting representative on the Council from among individual members on the basis of one representative per 10 individual members.

More usually, you have to wait to be invited by the management committee as an observer. They might ask you to leave when certain items arise, like staff pay. If you're there by invitation, you would have to comply, but, if any member of the group may attend, you could refuse unless the constitution actually covered this point. You probably would not have the right to speak, although the chair might give you permission, and you would not have a vote.

Some statutory bodies, like council committees and health authorities, have a duty to let the public into their meetings, except when they've decided that some particular business is confidential. Some get round this by deciding at the beginning of their meetings that everything is confidential. The 1982 Local Government Act is the one to quote if you are having problems with a council, or the Public Bodies (Admissions to Meetings) Act 1962 for the health service.

Staff members

Usually the paid workers of an organization are allowed to attend, but not to vote. If it is a charity, the Charity Commissioners will not let them. In some cases, staff are not even allowed to attend. In others, they can attend except while their conditions of service are being discussed.

One constitution says:

> The members of staff shall have the right to attend Council meetings and shall arrange to elect two voting representatives on the Council.

Arrangement of meetings

The constitution, or perhaps an attached schedule (see p. 5) should say:

- how often the management/executive committee should meet; the Gateway says 'not less than four times a year'. This allows you to meet more often if you want. Other constitutions say 'at least once each calendar month'.
- who must call the meetings. Usually this is the secretary, but often if s/he doesn't do so there is the power for two or three members of the committee either to do it themselves, or to require the secretary to carry out the duties.
- how much notice has to be given. Often this is seven days, although there may be a clause saying that so long as everyone agrees, a meeting can be called at shorter notice, perhaps to deal with an emergency. The Resource Project also has a clause saying that 'the accidental omission to give such notice to, or the non-receipt of such notice by any person shall not invalidate the proceedings of any such meeting'. This is quite common, and means that if the secretary forgets to post one or two letters, or if the Post Office fails to deliver them, the meeting can still go ahead. There is usually also a power to 'waive', that is, ignore, this requirement if everyone agrees.
- what is to be covered in the notice. The Resource Project says it must specify 'the place, the day and the time of the meeting and the nature of the business to be discussed'. Again this is standard. It doesn't mean the business has to be set out in very great detail, but that a general picture has to be given. The constitution may say in another section, however, that certain things, for example, resolutions or amendments to the constitution or the rules, can't be discussed unless they have been sent out with the notice, although there will usually be a special arrangement for emergencies. The list of business to be

discussed is called the **agenda**; there's an example of one on p. 86. It's covered in more detail in Chapter 4.

- how many people must be there before the meeting can take place. This is called the 'quorum'. This is a Latin word meaning 'of whom'. Apparently it originates from very old documents which would say, for example, that 'The Committee has twelve members at least four **of whom** must be present.'

Having a quorum stops a small unrepresentative group taking over by being the only ones to turn up, perhaps after not publicizing the meetings. The usual quorum for a committee is about one-third of its members. If it's a joint committee, say, of management and workers, then often each side will have to have a quorum to ensure that one group can't simply turn up and push things through while the others aren't there.

If meetings have continual trouble getting a quorum, this is usually a sign that something else is wrong; either the information is not getting out, or the meeting is not interesting enough for people to bother with.

The rules will usually say what is to happen if there is no quorum. For instance, the Gateway rules say:

> The quorum for a meeting of the Management Committee shall be four. If within half an hour of the appointed time for the meeting a quorum is not present the meeting shall stand adjourned until the same day of the following week at the same time and place. At such adjourned meeting the quorum shall be the same as that specified above.

The word 'quorum' has spawned more jargon. If your meeting has enough people, it is said to be 'quorate'. If there are not enough, then it is 'inquorate'.

The way that meetings of the management or executive committee are to be run may also be included in the constitution; or it might be in a separate set of standing orders. This is covered in detail in Chapters 2 and 3.

Voting

The rules will tell you what procedure is to be used for voting at both management committees and general meetings. The various procedures are explained in Chapter 4. They will also tell you who has a vote, and how many votes each person has.

Consider these points:

- Is the procedure the same for motions and elections, or different?
- Is a motion passed when it is voted for by a majority of those present; a majority of those voting; or a two-thirds majority of those present or voting? This can make a big difference to the chances of success for any particular proposal. Often, a proposal to reverse a previous decision needs a two-thirds majority, while a new proposal or question needs only a simple majority of those present. You will find more details on this on p. 48.
- If someone is representing a number of people, do they have extra votes according to those numbers? At trade-union conferences, for instance, a person representing a branch of 100 members may have one vote, and a person who represents 500 members might have five votes. On the other hand, at any Labour Party general committee, each person has only one vote; the different numbers in each branch are reflected in the fact that a big branch has more representatives than a small one.
- Can people appoint someone else to vote on their behalf? This is called 'proxy' voting, and is explained on p. 15. A proxy will usually have to be given in writing; it may be for just one meeting, or for a series.
- The position of the chair. Can s/he vote normally? Does s/he have a 'casting vote', that is, a vote to break a deadlock if there are equal numbers on each side? If so, is this in addition to, or instead of, his/her normal vote?

The Resource Project constitution says:

(i) Matters arising at any meeting of the management Committee shall be decided by the votes of a majority of members present and voting;
(ii) Each member shall have one vote;
(iii) In the case of an equality of votes the Chairperson on the meeting shall be entitled to a second or casting vote.

Payments

In commercial companies, the directors are paid often substantial amounts. In political and voluntary organizations, their equivalents are the management committee, and it would be very unusual for them to be paid. There is often a rule forbidding it; for instance the Gateway rules say: 'No member of the Management Committee shall derive any pecuniary benefit from the Centre and no member shall be appointed to any office in the Centre for which he would be entitled to receive payment for his services.

There may, however, be a rule allowing reasonable expenses to be paid back. So, for example, people who have travelled some distance or who needed to pay a babysitter for an evening meeting could be paid for this. Often people aren't aware that they can claim such expenses and it may put off low-paid or unemployed people from taking an active part; so it is important to make sure that this rule, if it exists, is publicized.

In trade unions, rules often lay down a specific scale of expenses, which may include a subsistence allowance, loss of earnings and sometimes a delegation fee. They may also give the procedure for claiming it. The NUPE rule says:

> Executive Council members shall be allowed the following expenses when engaged in the Council's business:
> loss of wages actually incurred;
> second-class travelling expenses;
> £4.50 per day except at weekends when the payment shall be £9 per day;
> subsistence allowance of £4 per journey for the inward and outward journeys (excepting members travelling less than fifty miles each way, who shall receive £2.25 per journey);
> £17 if required to stay overnight;
> £5 per day when representing the Union on International delegations.

As this rule says they are eligible for this 'when engaged in the Council's business', they would be paid the same amount if, say, they were addressing a branch meeting on the union's behalf.

Minutes

These are the notes of what happened at the meeting of the management committee, subcommittees and any general meetings. Examples of the way they are written are given on pp. 97–8. The rules will usually say they must be kept; they may also say that there has to be a **minute book**, to be kept in the office, or by the secretary, as a permanent record. It's usually the secretary's job to keep the minutes, although this is not always spelt out in the rules.

If the rules say minutes must be kept, and you have not done so, then if a legal query arose you could be in trouble, not only concerning that particular issue but also because the organization was not being run properly. Legally, all you need to record is the **decisions**, but frequently the minutes also include something about the discussion. See Chapter 10 for an explanation of the law on this.

Annual general meetings

Branches of national bodies, like trade unions and political parties, and groups like tenants' associations will usually have arrangements for calling meetings of all their members. Any organization that is a **company** must have a meeting of shareholders at least once a year. At national level, political parties, trade unions and some pressure groups have general meetings of **delegates** from the members. For instance, GMBATU hold an annual meeting, its conference, each year, to which its regions send delegates in proportion to their size.

Every organization, however, will have one formal meeting a year, whether of members or delegates; that is called the **annual general meeting**. At this, reports are given to the members about what has been happening over the last year and people are told what has been done with their money. Elections are held for the officers and the committee for the next year; alternatively, there might be a postal vote with the results announced at the meeting.

The constitution will tell you at what time of year the AGM must be called, how much notice is to be given to the members, and what has to be dealt with. It is often laid down that only business which people have been forewarned about can be dealt with, so a person can't turn up with a handwritten motion denouncing all the officers and get it passed the same evening.

NUPE's rules say:

> No Business other than that which appears on the Agenda shall be dealt with by conference except as provided for in standing order 13(a) [which allows for emergencies].

General meetings usually need a **quorum**. This might be about a tenth of the members, or a smaller proportion for a big organization. However, in some trade-union branches, a meeting that is to **mandate** the delegate for conference has no quorum, so that even if a very few people turn up, the meeting still takes place. This is to ensure that the member is told which way to vote, even if it is only by a very few other members, rather than having to reply on his/her own judgement.

The constitution may spell out what is to be considered at the annual meeting. The model constitution produced by the Northern Ireland Council of Social Services says:

> The Annual General Meeting will be held at such time, and date as the Management Committee shall determine, provided that the interval between one AGM and the next shall not exceed 15

calendar months, and that 21 clear days' notice in writing of the meeting shall have been sent to all members of the Association.

The Annual General Meeting will transact the following business:

(1) minutes of the previous AGM;

(2) consideration of the Annual Report prepared by the Committee;

(3) consideration of the Annual Audited Statement of Accounts;

(4) election of Honorary Officers and Management Committee;

(5) any other relevant business.

Alternatively, you may have to deduce from the rest of the clauses in that section or schedule what is covered. NUPE's rules, for instance, do not say specifically that the annual conference may deal with motions, but as it goes on at length about how a motion comes to be discussed, they are clearly assuming that they will be sent in.

Motions

If an AGM does deal with motions (which are explained in more detail on pp. 37–51), the constitution will also say how they get there, that is: whom you have to send them to; by what date; when and how they must be sent out to the members.

So one small trade union's rules say:

> The Executive Council or any two members may require the General Secretary to place on the Agenda any motion or motions. Each requisition must be made to the General Secretary at least three weeks before the date fixed for the Annual General Meeting, and the General Secretary shall send to all members the Final Agenda including all proposed motions . . . at least seven days before the time fixed for such meeting.

A larger organization might have a more elaborate procedure, because the motion would first of all have to go through a branch (this is explained in more detail on p. 142).

NUPE's rules say:

12. Motions and Amendments

(a) All motions for the agenda must be national and not local or regional in character. They must be signed by the chairman/woman and secretary of the branch, stamped with the branch stamp and sent to the General Secretary not later than 31st December preceding the Conference. A branch shall not submit

> more than two motions for the Preliminary Agenda of National Conference, nor shall a branch submit more than two amendments to items listed on the Preliminary Agenda for inclusion in the Final Agenda.

Calling an AGM

There is usually a rule about what happens if the secretary does not get around to calling the AGM. A specified number of other members would generally have the power to do it themselves, perhaps by advertising in the papers. One clause says:

> If in any year no Annual General Meeting is called within eighteen months of the last such meeting, an Annual General Meeting may be called by any two members by advertisement in the [local newspapers], giving at least 30 days' notice of the time and place of such meeting, and a meeting so called shall be a valid Annual General Meeting for all purposes including the election of officers.

Special or extraordinary meetings

Most organizations also have arrangements for 'special' or 'extraordinary' meetings to be called if there is a particular reason, or if members are concerned about something specific. Using the word 'extraordinary' may make it sound as if something earth-shattering has happened; in fact often these meetings are called for technical, non-controversial reasons. For instance, you might have required the agreement of the Charity Commissioners before you could change a rule, so that there was no chance to do this at the annual general meeting; however, two months later they wrote to say that it was all right, so, rather than wait until next year, you decided to make the rule change straight away. Of course, if something major is happening in your organization, it will probably involve at least one special general meeting.

■ In NALGO, 50 branches must send in identical resolutions calling for a special conference to discuss a particular item. The conference has to be held within a certain number of weeks. In 1984, for the first time ever, this power was used to try to prevent the union giving financial support to the National Union of Mineworkers in their strike, but this was voted down.

There will be a rule in the constitution saying how a special or extraordinary meeting is to be called.

The Gateway rules say:

A Special General Meeting of the Centre shall be convened by the Secretary at the request of the Management Committee or upon a requisition being delivered to him signed by at least ten registered members. Notice of such Special Meeting shall be given by him to all registered members of the Centre and such meeting shall be held within fifteen days after the receipt by him of such a requisition.

Every requisition for a Special Meeting of the Centre shall state the business proposed to be transacted at the Special Meeting.

If the Secretary fails to act upon such a requisition for a Special Meeting any five of those members who signed the requisition may convene the Special Meeting giving not less than fourteen days' notice of the date, time, and place and of the business proposed to be transacted at the proposed meeting, by public advertisement in a local newspaper and by such other means as is reasonably practicable to bring it to the notice of all registered members.

Accounts

In a limited company, the rules must say that proper accounts will be kept; most other sets of rules will stipulate this; they will usually say that this is the treasurer's job, although in a large organization there will be paid staff to do it and the treasurer will only have to supervise.

Companies have to keep their accounts in a specified form, laid down by the Companies Act, and have to send copies into Companies House. Anyone who volunteers to keep accounts should make sure they understand the duties. Look at *How to Manage Your Money, If You Have Any* or *Accounting and Financial Management for Charities* (details of both in Further Reading on p. 210) for help on this.

Charities have to send copies of their accounts to the Charity Commissioners and unions must send them to the Certification Officer. If the council, or another charity, is giving you a grant, it is likely to want to see the accounts too, but this may not be written into the rules; instead it might be laid down as a condition in the letter giving you the grant.

The rules usually lay down that the accounts can be inspected by any member. NUPE's rule says: 'Every person having an interest in the funds of the union may, on giving reasonable notice, inspect all the books of the union and see the names of the members.'

In addition, the accounts will almost always have to be presented to the annual general meeting for approval. Usually this is after they have been **audited**.

A trade union, a company or a housing association must have

audited accounts by law. In business, the auditor is the outside accountant who comes in to check the company's accounts, which will have already been drawn up by an employee, and confirm that everything is in order.

Trade unions, certainly at national level, will also have their accounts audited by professionals; so should any organization with a large turnover of funds, possibly because it is paying staff out of a grant, or collecting rent and using it for repairs. If the council, or some other organization, gives your group a grant, it may specify what qualifications your auditor must have. S/he might have to be a chartered accountant, for instance.

In a small group, or the local branch of a political party or a union, the auditors may be volunteers without any formal training, but they are doing the same job; s/he is there to double-check that no one has gone off to Bermuda with the proceeds of the last jumble sale. The auditors are usually formally elected at the AGM. The Northern Ireland Council of Social Services model constitution says, for example: 'The annual statement of accounts must be produced at the Annual General Meeting, properly audited, by two auditors elected at the AGM, and who shall not be members of the committee.'

Unions tend to be particularly strict about the requirement to audit accounts.

NUPE's rules say:

> The accounts and other documents of each branch shall be examined quarterly by two auditors (not serving in any other paid capacity) who shall be elected at each annual meeting by a majority of the members present . . .
>
> The auditors shall have access to all branch books, documents, receipts for payments, including payments to Head Office and receipts for branch officers' expenses due for the previous quarter, in order to conduct the audit, which must be done in time to enable the secretary to make his/her return to the General Secretary at the appointed time.
>
> Before signing the branch cash sheet the auditors must satisfy themselves as to the arithmetical accuracy of the various documents, see that the financial aspects of these rules have been complied with, and ensure that the cash sent to Head Office, plus the cash in hand, is the correct amount accounted for and that the branch cash sheet is an accurate record of the branch's financial state.

The seal

One other clause that might puzzle you, if you are a limited company, is the reference to a 'seal'. This is an official emblem of the group, which you use to emboss formal documents like a lease or a mortgage. The rules will say who should look after it, and who can authorize it to be used. Usually the secretary will keep it and the management committee authorize its use.

Altering the rules

Any constitution should say how it can be altered. Usually there's a special procedure, or some way in which it is rather more difficult to take this decision than some others. So, for example, NUPE says that its rules can only be changed at a rules revision conference held every other year, or by a ballot of all its members. The Resource Project says there must be a majority vote of three-quarters of the people present at a general meeting and that the notice of this meeting must specify what change is to be made. Voluntary groups may also require the agreement of the bodies that provide grants, as well as the Charity Commissioners. The approvals you have to get should be listed in the rules, but are not always.

The rules of a branch of a national body, like a union or the Labour Party, will be laid down at national level and its powers to alter them will be very limited. The Labour Party, for instance, only allows its local parties to decide how many delegates attend its meetings and in which month its AGM will be held; everything else is fixed nationally.

Winding up

The rule on this may be called 'Dissolution' or 'Termination'. It should say what the procedure is for winding up and what happens to any assets that are left. So, for instance, the NUPE rules say that 'The Union may be dissolved by the votes of five-sixths of its financial members', and the Resource Project says that any property left after paying off debts should be transferred to another organization, 'having objects similar to the objects of the Project and a rule or constitution prohibiting the distribution of property or profits directly or indirectly'.

DIY constitutions

A small friendly group that's just setting up or that has quite limited aims – for instance, as a discussion group – does not need a formal constitution at all. But, as pointed out on p. 6, once things become more complicated and you find yourselves employing staff, holding property or having branches or sub-groups, you will need some sort of formal document to satisfy other people like the bank manager.

Groups vary a good deal in their approach to this. CND does not impose any sort of framework on its local groups, while the Labour Party insists that you adopt the full constitution before you can be recognized as a real branch. This can create considerable problems, for instance, for women's sections who do not want to operate within the very hierarchical framework laid down.

Drawing up your own constitution, however, can be an agonizing experience, as you get sidetracked in discussion of tiny points about the running of the group, rather than getting on with the actual business.

It can also expose the differences of view you have so far successfully papered over, because when you come to discuss the 'aims and objectives' clause you have to begin to define exactly what you are doing. This may be a good thing, since it clarifies the picture for people who have perhaps become involved without thinking too much about why. On the other hand, many successful groups have people within them with quite opposed ideas, and manage by not exploring them too deeply. Rather than starting from scratch, therefore, you may wish to adopt a 'model' constitution, since there are a number around (the Further Reading on p. 210 suggests some places to look), or you can borrow one from an organization similar to yours.

Whether you decide to start from scratch or adapt someone else's version, use the checklist on pp. 33–5 to make sure you include everything and that the constitution is suitable for your group. Decide first of all on **how** you want to operate and build the various clauses round that, remembering that this is a legal document that has to satisfy bank managers and perhaps also solicitors who are used to formal methods of working. So you may not be able to put in everything you want, but you can word the clauses in such a way that you can quite legitimately operate as you intend.

■ Mary's group intend to rotate the chair at each meeting (see p. 64). They therefore put in a clause which says that 'The Chair shall be appointed by the committee at such intervals as the Committee decide.' This means that, if the committee decides to appoint a new chair at every meeting, they are still acting legally.

Chapter 10 explains the legal problems you can run into if you are not operating in line with the letter of your constitution.

If you want a bank manager to let you open an account or anyone to give you a grant, you need:

- a statement of your aims and objectives, including the powers to do the things you plan to do;
- rules about keeping minutes and accounts;
- a description of who can be a member;
- a description of how the committee is appointed;
- a description of how the rules may be changed;
- a procedure for winding up the organization.

You can put in grant applications or apply for an account without such a constitution, calling yourselves a 'steering committee' and saying that it will be sent in as soon as it is finalized; but you are unlikely actually to be paid money until it is complete.

There is no need for all this to be written in legal language. It can be in plain English, but it must be clear and precise, not woolly.

Checklist

Use this to go through the various documents; make a note in the spaces provided about where each item is covered, and put down the answers to the various questions.

clause in your rules

What sort of organization are you?
- an unincorporated association (pp. 2–3) ____________
- a company limited by guarantee (pp. 2–3) ____________
- a co-operative registered as an
  - Industrial and Provident Society (pp. 2–3) ____________
  - or as a Friendly Society (pp. 2–3) ____________
- a company limited by shares (pp. 2–3) ____________
- a trade union (pp. 2–3) ____________

Are you a charity? Yes/no (p. 3) ____________
Have you got trustees? Yes/no (p. 3) ____________
Have you got
- a constitution (p. 2) ____________
- a rule book (p. 2) ____________
- a trust deed (pp. 3–4) ____________
- a Memorandum and Articles (p. 3) ____________
- standing orders (Chap. 2) ____________

Is there a definitions clause? (p. 5) ____________
What does the objects (or aims and objectives) clause say? (pp. 6–7) ____________
Do you have powers to:
- own land? (pp. 6–7) ____________
- employ staff? (pp. 6–7) ____________
- borrow money? (pp. 6–7) ____________

What restrictions are there on what you can do? (pp. 6–7) ____________

Membership

Who can belong to your organization? (pp. 7–11) ____________
Do they have to buy shares? (p. 7) ____________
Can anyone be a member? (p. 8) ____________
How can people be excluded? (p. 8) ____________
Can people be expelled? (pp. 9–10) ____________
Do you have honorary, associate or affiliate members? (p. 8) ____________
How much is the subscription? (pp. 10–11) ____________
How do you change the subscription? (p. 10) ____________
If you don't pay the subscription, how long does it take before you lose your membership rights? (p. 11) ____________

clause in your rules

Management committee

Who are the management committee (executive committee, executive council are alternative names)? (pp. 11–13) ____________
How many people sit on it? (p. 13) ____________
How long is their term of office? (p. 13) ____________
Who can nominate them? (p. 13) ____________
What are the time limits for nominating? (p. 13) ____________
Who can vote for them? (p. 14) ____________
When do you vote for them? (pp. 14–15) ____________
What's the procedure? (pp. 14–15) ____________
Are proxy votes allowed? (pp. 14–15) ____________
Are there any co-opted people? (pp. 15–16) ____________
What happens if a committee member doesn't come to meetings? (p. 17) ____________
What are the powers of the committee? (pp. 17–18) ____________
Can they have subcommittees? (pp. 18–19) ____________
What are they allowed to do? (pp. 18–19) ____________
Who are the officers? (pp. 19–20) ____________
What are they allowed to do? (pp. 19–20) ____________
When do the committee meet? (p. 21) ____________
How much notice do you get of meetings? (p. 21) ____________
Are observers allowed at the committee meetings? (p. 20) ____________

Annual general meetings (AGMs)

When do you have your AGMs? (pp. 25–8) ____________
Who is allowed to come? (pp. 25–7) ____________
What business must it deal with? (pp. 25–7) ____________
Can it pass resolutions? (p. 26) ____________
When must they be sent in? (pp. 26–7) ____________
To whom? (pp. 26–7) ____________
What's the quorum? (p. 25) ____________
What happens if the secretary doesn't call an AGM (p. 27) ____________

Special meetings

How do you call a special meeting? (pp. 27–8) ____________
How much notice must be given? (pp. 27–8) ____________
What business can it deal with? (pp. 27–8) ____________
What's the quorum? (pp. 27–8) ____________

clause in
your rules

Arrangements at meetings

Are staff allowed to attend? (pp. 20–21) ____________
Can they vote? (pp. 20–21) ____________
What's the voting procedure? (pp. 22–3) ____________
What's the rule about majorities? (p. 23) ____________
Can anyone be paid for attending? (pp. 23–4) ____________
Who keeps the minutes? (pp. 24–5) ____________
Is there a rule about a minute book? (pp. 24–5) ____________

Is there a rule about keeping accounts? (p. 28) ____________
Who is to audit the accounts? (p. 29) ____________
When? (p. 29) ____________
Where are the accounts to be sent? (p. 29) ____________
How do you alter the rules? (p. 30) ____________
Who must approve the alterations? (p. 30) ____________
How do you wind up the organization? (p. 31) ____________
Do you need an official seal? (pp. 29–30) ____________
Who looks after it? (pp. 29–30) ____________
Have you got trustees? (p. 3) ____________
Who are they? (p. 3) ____________
Is there an indemnity clause for them? (p. 3) ____________

2.

Standing orders

The standing orders of a group are the set of rules about how its meetings are to be run. Your group may have a set of standing orders included in the constitution, or they may be written separately. Try to have it next to you while reading this chapter, which will start by going through the standing orders of various groups, using them as examples to show what is usual practice and also where there can be variations.

Many groups do not have a set of rules covering every question, or indeed any at all. The GMBATU, the country's third biggest union, has no standing orders for its annual conference. It manages without them by basing its procedures on unwritten rules that have developed over the years. You may therefore need to ask experienced people about some of the points covered here, if nothing is written down.

Having looked at the formal arrangements, this chapter will go on to look at how many of these procedures you actually need, and whether there are better ways of running things. It then looks at possible alternatives, especially for groups that are committed to a non-hierarchical way of organizing themselves, and want to get all the members involved, rather than only a small committee.

Explaining the standing orders also involves explaining much of the ordinary procedures of meetings. Those parts which are not covered here are in Chapter 4, on procedures, and there are checklists at the end of the chapter which cover points raised by both.

It is useful to look at the way standing orders have developed, because they tend to follow a rigid pattern that has been laid down by two 'experts', Hannington and Citrine.

These are the authors of two books about the way to run meetings, which traditionalists in the labour movement regard as their bibles. Both books are now quite old; they both assume that if meetings are not being run along the lines they lay down, they are not proper meetings – whatever their size, and whatever the reasons for having the meetings. The books are written for organizations that have a complete collection of officers, and they take it for granted that the chair is going to be a man, and probably a man of at least middle age.

The first of these books is called *Mr Chairman* (see Further Reading on p. 210). It is by Wal Hannington, who, in the 1930s, was a major leader in the unemployed movement; judging by the book, he grew a lot more conservative as he got older. It was written in the 1950s and has been reprinted several times since. Its first paragraph says: 'From the moment that the meeting opens, whether public or private, to the time that it closes, the Chairman has the responsibility for seeing that it is conducted in an orderly and business like manner', and it continues in this vein.

The second book is even more firmly embedded in the labour movement: Citrine's *ABC of Chairmanship* (see Further Reading). Citrine was General Secretary of the TUC from 1926 to 1946. The first version of his book was published in 1921 as *The Labour Chairman* and then revised in 1939 under its new title. He revised it in 1943 and 1952, and it was largely rewritten in 1982 by Norman Citrine and Michael Cannell. To say that something is 'according to Citrine' is usually enough to settle an argument in the Labour Party or trade unions. The standing orders of the Writers' Guild, for instance, say that 'other than by the above, the meeting shall be conducted and matters of order and procedure settled in accordance with *The ABC of Chairmanship* by Citrine'. There is a set of model standing orders at the back of Citrine's book which many organizations have adopted.

Not many people today actually read these books closely. If they did, they would realize that in a number of ways groups do stray from them, even the Labour Party and the TUC, when the procedure suggested is too cumbersome or lacks common sense. However, because you may well be working with a chair who has swallowed the books whole, this chapter points out where they differ from the way meetings usually operate.

Arrangements for the meeting

The standing orders will begin by laying down the arrangements: the time the meeting must start, the time it must finish, and possibly also the place where the meeting is held.

They may also say what is to be on the **agenda**, that is, the list of things to be discussed (explained further on p. 85).

Motions

A motion is a proposal, put formally to the meeting, for people to agree or disagree with. It is then voted on if there are people who disagree with it. If it is passed, it becomes a 'resolution' and the policy of the organization; perhaps it authorizes the officers to spend some money or take some action; or it might tell the executive committee that they were wrong about something that has already happened.

At a meeting of individuals, an individual can put forward a motion. If, however, it is a meeting of delegates from branches or groups, or affiliated organizations, the motion usually has to come from the branch or group and be proposed (see p. 39) by a delegate from it.

For example, Charles Sims wants to change the council's policy on building tower blocks. So he puts forward a motion at the meeting of Balham branch of the party. When it's passed, it is then called a resolution and is sent by the secretary of the branch to the party secretary. Charles, as a **delegate** to the party meeting, then proposes it on behalf of the whole branch. It might then be sent further up the line, to the District Labour Party.

Some organizations have rules about what subjects can be covered in motions, particularly when it comes to conferences. So for instance at the NUPE national conference, all motions 'must be national and not local or regional in character'. The Labour Party says that motions must not deal with more than one subject and, if a subject has been discussed one year, it cannot be discussed again until three years have passed. A motion that deals with a forbidden subject is ruled 'out of order' by the standing orders committee. See p. 150 for an explanation of this.

Motions usually begin 'That this conference' or 'This meeting' and then say what the proposal is. Try to write your motion so that you say first what you are supporting, or opposing, and then what you intend to do about it.

Often motions are very long, listing all the arguments for support or opposition. This is a habit particularly of left-wing groups, who persist in the view that a motion 200 words long must be twice as good as one that is only 100 words long. This is a mistake; the motion loses its impact and people get bored reading it all the way through. It's more sensible to give the arguments in the speeches about the motion, rather than writing them all down. A short punchy statement is much more attractive to the people you are trying to convert.

Notice

In many organizations you have to give notice, that is, tell people in advance of any motion. It may have to be sent to the secretary a few days before, in time for it to be put on the agenda. In smaller organizations, you may have to hand a copy of the motion in writing to the secretary at the beginning of the meeting, or you may simply have to say what you are proposing at the start of the discussion.

The standing orders for a committee or subcommittee usually don't require advance notice. There is usually a special exemption for **emergency** motions on this. One trade union, for instance, says that motions have to be received by the secretary at least three weeks before a general meeting, but that

> any motion received after the last date for receipt of motions as determined in Rule 10(b) can be included in the final agenda if such motion deals with urgent items. The validity as to whether the motion(s) is urgent or is of an emergency nature is at the discretion of the meeting.

Emergency motions

Emergency motions are generally allowed where something has happened since the last date on which it was possible to put a motion forward in the usual way and where the question is sufficiently important for people to think it cannot wait. Before it can be discussed, the meeting has to agree that it is an emergency. It could be turned down at this stage because it has been overtaken by events if the situation has developed fast.

■ The Eversley branch meets on the second Wednesday in each month. The Americans invade Grenada after the branch meeting has taken place, so a person from Eversley can put forward an emergency motion at the next general meeting, without having to go through the branch. On the other hand, one of the Labour councillors decided to buy her council house two months ago, but no one mentioned it at the branch meeting. When an Eversley member puts up an emergency motion on this, it is ruled out of order because it could have been dealt with in the ordinary way.

Someone else puts up a motion about the party's attitude to Greenham Common, and the MP gets up and explains that the leader made a statement in the House of Commons that day on it. So the meeting decides the motion doesn't apply any more, and refuses to discuss it.

Proposing and seconding

Standing orders usually say that a motion must be proposed and seconded before the discussion starts. The person putting it forward is the proposer; at least one other must express his or her support for it as the seconder. The idea of this is that the group need not waste its time discussing items about which only one person feels strongly and for which there is no support. The person putting forward the motion is allowed to state his or her argument, and then the person in the chair asks: 'Is that motion seconded?' In a big conference the seconder will usually have been arranged beforehand. At an ordinary meeting, if no one speaks or raises a hand the motion **falls**, that is, it won't be discussed. If you want to make sure there is a discussion, therefore, you have to tip someone off in advance to second you. Some groups don't allow the proposer even to state the argument unless the motion is seconded, but this is rare.

Here is an example to explain the usual procedure.

■ Peter Pickard comes to his ward meeting with a motion about a local strike. He gives a copy to the secretary at the beginning of the meeting and the secretary reads it out then. When the item 'Motions' is reached on the agenda, Peter stands up and says, 'I propose the motion That this meeting support the strikers and all members agree to donate £5 a week to the hardship fund.' Peter explains why and then the person in the chair asks, 'Is that motion seconded?' Jane Cooper puts her hand up and says, 'I second it.' She then explains why she supports it, and then the chair asks for people to speak in favour or against the motion. Jane could say, 'I second it **formally**', which means she has chosen not to speak at that time. In an ordinary meeting, you can add that you 'reserve the right' to speak later. This wouldn't be allowed at a big conference, where there is a queue of speakers; there, if you didn't speak at the beginning of the debate, you would lose your chance.

In a small committee or group, people don't usually demand a seconder before the debate begins; in fact, often you have the discussion first and then someone produces a motion which seems in line with the views expressed.

Amendments

Using the above example of Peter Pickard's motion, perhaps Lorraine O'Grady is fully in support of the strikers, but knows that many of the branch members could not afford £5 a week. What can she do? She puts forward an **amendment**, which changes the details of the motion but retains the principle. Lorraine might say, 'I propose an amendment to **delete** £5 and insert £1.' She would need to be seconded.

An amendment is meant to be on the same subject as the motion, and should not directly contradict it. If it does, it is called a 'direct negative' and is ruled out of order on the grounds that, if you want to oppose the motion, you vote against it, rather than messing about with it. It would also be ruled out of order if it was irrelevant to the motion. If the chair thinks an amendment does not fit in with the rules or standing orders, s/he can rule it **out of order** (see p. 43).

For a conference you usually have also to **give notice** of amendments, as you do with motions. This is explained in detail on p. 144.

For a smaller meeting, though, it's usual for amendments to be allowed 'from the floor', that is, someone can simply propose one during the discussion. According to Citrine, at an ordinary meeting, only one amendment should be 'on the floor', that is, under discussion, at any one time. Many organizations follow this. This reduces the confusion, but it can also make the discussion very long-winded and it may mean that you go over the same ground several times. A group that does this usually allows you to let people know if you want to put forward a different amendment. So Jill Connor might say, while the meeting was discussing Lorraine's amendment, 'I think £5 is too high and £1 is too low. I therefore want to give notice that I will be moving a further amendment to delete £5 and insert £2.50.' In this case, you would have a vote about the £1 amendment, then have another discussion about the £2.50 amendment.

Many other groups, however, have all the amendments put forward at once and then the discussion ranges over all of them. At the end, therefore, you have a series of votes on the different amendments. If there are several, they can either be taken in the order in which they are put forward, or in the order in which they fit into the motion. There is an example of how this works on p. 45.

Accepting amendments

What if one person puts up a motion and then another person comes along with a proposed change s/he likes better? Can that be included in the motion without a vote being taken? There can be problems with this, but the sensible rule is that, so long as the rules about giving notice or circulating the amendment have been followed, the mover is allowed to accept an amendment, and therefore change the motion, **before** the discussion starts, but not once the meeting has begun talking about it.

Citrine says that at this point the motion 'becomes the property of the meeting'. What he means is that to make a change at this point can be unfair and misleading. Taking Peter's example again, if halfway through the debate he accepted another amendment to call a general strike, it would mean that those people who supported the strikers but thought that a general strike called by the Labour Party in Fenwick-on-Avon would be a disastrous flop would have no chance to propose a different amendment or vote against the idea; they might feel they had to vote against the whole motion because of this. The mover, therefore, should only be allowed to accept an amendment if no one objects to it, and the chair should specifically stipulate that. If there are objections, there should be a vote.

Withdrawing amendments (or motions)

The same rule should apply if someone wants to withdraw an amendment. If there are several near-identical motions or amendments, you may as well get some of them out of the way before the discussion starts, but not after that, because again it can be unfair. If Peter doesn't like the way his motion has been amended, he might not want to have his name on it any more, and he might try to withdraw it, that is, simply drop it. This would mean people can't discuss it and make their views known.

If motions are **composited** (see p. 150), then technically other ones are withdrawn in favour of the new composite.

Speaking

It is common for the rules to say that people must stand up when speaking to a meeting; although this would be too formal for a small meeting, for a large one it does mean you can be heard better. It also makes it less likely that there will be backchat and other conversations going on around you, as it will be clear that only one person is supposed to speak at any one time. It is said that the person 'has the floor'. The rules often say also that you must give your name at the beginning of your speech.

There is usually a time limit on the length of speeches. NUPE, for instance, says that proposers at its conference can speak for up to 10 minutes, everyone else for up to five, and that 'a bell will be rung when these times expire'. It is the job of the chair to enforce the time limit, and to be sure to do it fairly.

Another set of standing orders says that no one – except the proposer, who has a 'right of reply' (see p. 44) – can speak twice on any item; but for this purpose each motion and amendment is counted as a separate item. This sort of limit is quite frequent, but, often, where the motion and amendments are taken in one debate, you can speak only once in that particular debate. This is explained in more detail on p. 165 in the chapter on conferences.

Interruptions

Usually once people are speaking, they must not be interrupted except on a **point of order** (explained in the next section).

So one trade-union rule book states:

> No member shall interrupt another while he is speaking, except on a point of order; that is, to draw attention to some breach of the procedure of the meeting. Points of information or explanation concerning a speech may be accepted by the Chairman at his discretion as soon as the speech is finished.

In Parliament, from which much of the standard procedure is taken, there's a rule about interruptions to a speech. For instance, Fred Disney MP might be making a speech about sewers. Donald Mouse MP can stand up and wait for Fred Disney to notice him, or ask him, 'Will you give way?' If Fred wants to allow the interruption, he sits down, which is called 'giving way', and Donald makes his point and sits down again. If Fred thinks he has been interrupted too many times already, or he doesn't like interruptions, he says, 'I will not give way,' and Donald has to sit down.

This procedure is sometimes used in organizations that model themselves closely on Parliament, like debating societies, but it's not very usual.

Points of order

This is when someone says that the rules about the way the meeting is to be run are not being followed. It is different from saying something about the subject that's being discussed. Almost anything that is covered in standing orders can be raised as a point of order, and you can say something either about the way the chair is running the meeting, or about what one of the members is doing or saying.

So, for example, someone could raise a point about:

- whether you can deal with a subject that people did not know was coming up;
- whether a particular amendment to a motion should be taken first or last (see p. 45);
- whether you can start the meeting at all, if not enough people are there to form a quorum (see p. 25).

A point of order can also be raised about 'unparliamentary' or 'objectionable' language. This means comments that are personally offensive, or, for example, swearing at someone. Saying openly that someone there is corrupt or dishonest would usually count as objectionable. Someone might say, 'Is it in order to call comrade X a four-eyed git?' This rule is intended to keep the peace and keep tempers down. In fact, people can be just as rude in 'parliamentary language'; they simply wrap it up a little more.

You could use this rule also to object to sexist or racist language, although many traditionalists would not see this as correct.

A point of order **takes precedence**. That is, it interrupts whatever else is going on. When someone makes a point of order the chair should stop talking, or stop the current speaker, listen to what you've got to say, and then **make a ruling**. This means s/he decides whether what you're saying is right or wrong.

Points of information or explanation

This is supposed to be a short speech clarifying the facts or a previous statement. So, for instance, Jo Smith might say that last Wednesday he went to a meeting with management along with his colleagues, and Annie Jones might then say, if she felt it to be important, 'On a point of information, actually it was last Tuesday.'

A point of **personal explanation** is when something has been said about a person and they want to explain their view or defend themselves against an accusation they see as unfair. So someone might say that Oliver Sykes was wrong not to have attended a certain meeting; Oliver could stand up and say, 'On a point of personal explanation, the letter telling me about the meeting did not arrive at my house until the next day.' A chair usually allows people to make these, even if ordinary points of information are being ruled out.

Right of reply

After the discussion and before a vote is taken the person who originally put forward the motion has the **right of reply**. This means s/he can answer the opposition's arguments, and deal with any questions, perhaps about the facts of the case, that have come up. S/he is not supposed to 'introduce new material', that is, produce a whole lot of new arguments at this stage, because, since s/he is intended to be the last speaker, no one is going to be able to answer them. Citrine says that people moving amendments do not have the right of reply, but in fact groups usually do allow this.

Taking decisions

Returning to the example of Peter's motion, his proposal was that:

'This meeting support the strikers and all members agree to donate £5 a week to their hardship fund.'

Amendment A (Lorraine's) is to 'delete £5, insert £1'.

Amendment B (Jill's) is to 'delete £5, insert £2.50'.

Andy Bartlett has also proposed Amendment C: 'Insert after "strikers", "by all possible means including the calling of a general strike in Fenwick-on-Avon on Friday July 13".'

The meeting could vote on these in any order; it will be clearest if they take Andy's amendment (C) first, as it deals with the first line of the motion. The other two both deal with the same thing; so they take the one moved first, Lorraine's.

So the meeting votes on Amendment C, and there are more votes against than for, so it is **lost**. Amendment A is **carried**. Some people would then say this ruled out Amendment B, as you'd decided on that point. It would be quite possible, however, for people who wanted to reduce the figure from £5 to vote for Amendment A, but for them to be willing to pay a bit more than £1. In this case, therefore, the chair ought to have a vote on Amendment B. What matters is whether the result of agreeing to the next amendment would make the last one nonsensical. If so, it should be ruled out. The chair should make a clear ruling about this before the voting starts. Another example may help here.

David Cole moves Amendment D to Peter's motion. This is 'to add after "strikers", "but considers that this support should be limited to moral and financial help and there should be no call for sympathy action".'

If this was passed, as well as Andy's amendment, the two lines would contradict each other. The chair therefore says, before the vote is taken, 'I regard Amendments C and D as opposing each other. I'm taking Amendment C first, as it was moved first; if it is carried, we will not vote on Amendment D.'

The amendments that are passed or 'carried' are incorporated into the motion, which is then called the 'substantive' motion. You might have a further discussion on this and then the chair should ask you to vote for or against it. By now the motion may be quite different from the original, so the chair ought to read it out again, or put it on a blackboard, before people vote, to make sure they know what they are voting on. It is rather easy to forget to put the motion finally to the vote, if you've just gone through a whole series of amendments, but it is important. In the example we've just used, there might be people who didn't support the strikers at all and had been voting all the way through for amendments which would give the least amount of help to them; they now need the chance to express their views on the principle itself, rather than on the details. So the chair should say, 'Now please vote on the motion, which is . . . [reads it out]. Those in favour; those against.'

Voting

You don't have to vote on every motion. If no one disagrees, you may simply pass it with everyone muttering, 'Agreed.' The standing orders, however, will tell you **how** voting is to be done, when it is necessary. A union rule book, for instance, might say: 'All voting shall bc by membership card.' This means that when a vote is called for, everyone holds up their membership card, and a count is taken. If you have forgotten yours, you can't vote. NUPE's standing orders say that all voting at branch meetings is to be by **show of hands**. This means that when you come to vote, you put up your hand and hold it there until you've been counted. Sometimes you may have to hold up your **credential** (see p. 98) or your **agenda** (see p. 86) to show that you are entitled to vote. Other methods of voting which might be laid down in standing orders are:

- secret ballot. This can mean you mark a piece of paper, already printed with the names of the people, or the motion, you are voting about. Alternatively, you might have to write down on a piece of paper the names of those you want to vote for, or write 'For' or 'Against' if you're voting on a motion.
- roll-call vote. This is rare, but takes place at some very formal meetings like council meetings, or in cases where there might be a legal liability on people. The chair, or secretary, has to read out the names of each person entitled to vote, and then that person says, 'For,' or 'Against.' If they want to abstain, that is, not to vote at all, they usually have to leave the room altogether. The process is long, laborious and boring.
- card vote. This happens at big conferences, and is explained in detail on pp. 156–8.

Within each voting system, there are different ways of counting the votes, and these are dealt with on pp. 131–2.

At an ordinary meeting, voting on motions is usually by show of hands, and by secret ballot for elections.

Counting

It is the chair's job to count people and decide whether the motion is passed or not. S/he may find the votes are heavily on one side or the other. If so, s/he need not count, but simply 'declare the motion carried (or lost)'. A resolution can be carried in this way:

- unanimously, which means everyone voted for it;
- *nem. con.*, which is a shortening of two Latin words, meaning no one voted against it; so there might have been people abstaining, but they did not feel strongly enough to put up their hands against it;
- overwhelmingly, which means there were a few people against, but too few to matter.

However, if anyone protests against this, or if it is not clear who has won, the chair must count the hands. The secretary usually helps. It might be necessary also to appoint **tellers**, that is, other people to count as well.

Some standing orders say you must appoint tellers at the beginning of each meeting, and lay down a procedure for doing so. They will probably have to be proposed and seconded. If there has to be a vote on them, the chair and secretary must do the counting unaided. The usual practice, however, is not to bother to appoint tellers unless you need to. So at the start of a meeting where you know you are going to have a lot of elections, you do so, but not otherwise.

If you have a secret ballot, you will have to have tellers, because the papers will need to be counted in a separate room, and the chair and secretary can't do that while the meeting is going on. In some sets of standing orders these people are called 'scrutineers', but it means the same.

The people doing the counting should tell the chair what the figures are. If they come up with different results, they will have to count again, until everyone is satisfied. Then the chair makes an announcement, saying, 'I declare the motion carried (or lost) by 23 votes to 12.' The secretary then puts this result down in the minutes, so that everyone knows what has happened and can check back if necessary.

Abstentions

In some groups, it's usual also to count the people **abstaining**, that is, not voting either way. If so, they should be asked to put up their hands, after the people for and against have voted. In other groups this is felt to be a waste of time. If the chair is asked to count the abstentions, however, there would normally not be any good reason to refuse.

Casting vote

If there is a tie, the chair may have a **casting** vote, as was explained on p. 23. The idea of this is to make sure there will actually be a decision. This must be used separately from the chair's normal vote. S/he must vote first, or abstain, see if there is a deadlock, and only then use the casting vote.

Quite reasonably, standard practice is that the casting vote is not used to change policy. This is often called 'keeping the status quo'. If the change cannot get enough support on its own, it should not be voted through. So if the motion were that 'In future this branch will support CND', and there was a tie, the chair ought to vote against, whatever his/her views.

For **remitting** a motion, see p. 156.

Rescinding a motion

Sometimes a motion is passed almost accidentally and people only realize the implications afterwards, or the executive doesn't like the decision that's been taken, or the situation changes so that the motion is now unsuitable. Therefore there is usually a procedure for rescinding a motion, but it is made more difficult than passing the original motion, in order to stop people chopping and changing too often.

The procedure may say a motion cannot be rescinded within a certain time (say three months) of being passed. It could say you need a two-thirds majority to make the change, or indeed it could say both. To get round this, sometimes people propose motions that have the same effect but in a different way. For instance, someone might say, 'That no action be taken on the motion to call a general strike.'

Logically, a motion that rescinds another, even if it does not say so, should be treated in the same way. If someone objected to the motion, therefore, the chair should be asked to decide whether it is in order or not. This is called 'making a ruling' and is explained on pp. 55–7.

If a second motion is passed which contradicts the first, it should supersede it.

Procedural motions

The standing orders of most groups cover some, or all, of the 'procedural' motions that are beloved by bureaucrats and hated by the rest of us. These are motions that do not deal with the subject itself, but with the method of dealing with the subject. They include several methods of cutting down the length of time for discussion, or not taking a decision on a particular issue. They can sometimes be useful. There may be so much agreement that people see no point in going on discussing an issue and want to vote quickly; or the opposite situation may arise, where it's clear that the organization is going to split wide open if it is forced to vote on something and no one wants this, so everyone feels that it's better to duck the issue. More often, though, these procedural motions are used as a way of stifling discussion, and so need to be watched.

The first one is 'that the question (or motion) be now put'. This means that you consider the discussion has gone on long enough and you should vote on that item and move on to the next one. Usually it can't be proposed by someone who has already spoken in the discussion, as it is considered unfair that someone should use his or her chance to speak, and then try to shut other people up.

The TSSA rules say:

> If after discussion on any item, it is proposed and seconded 'that the question be now put', that motion must (if the Chairman accepts it) be voted on without any further discussion, and if carried the particular item in question must then be put to the vote after the mover of any resolution involved in that item has replied.

Returning to our example of Peter's motion on the local strike, therefore, assume that Peter has proposed his motion; it's been seconded and several other people have spoken, all in favour. Sandra Peers is impatient to get on to the next item, which is more controversial. She hasn't spoken in the debate. So she is entitled to ask 'that the motion be now put'.

The chair agrees to accept the motion (Citrine says that s/he can refuse if the member is being obstructive). Dave Hughes seconds it and the meeting then **votes on Sandra's motion**; there are no speeches about it, for or against. If it's lost, the debate carries on as before. If it's carried, then you have to start voting on the motion and amendments the debate is about. The proposer is allowed to reply to the points that have already been made, but no one else should speak.

Another procedural motion is '**next business**'. A typical union rule book says:

> A Full Member who believes that it is undesirable for the meeting to vote on any motion before it may move 'Next Business.' If this motion is accepted by the Chairman and seconded, by a full member, it shall at once be put to the vote. If it is carried, the motion before the meeting shall not be further discussed, nor voted upon, and the meeting will pass at once to the next item on

the agenda. 'Next Business' may not be moved by any member who has spoken in the debate which it seeks to cut short.

What does this mean? Changing the example, let us assume that Shiraz Jawali said something that was not in line with her branch's policy at a conference. People are quite angry, but as the debate proceeds it is obvious that she's under a lot of strain and is upset by the whole thing. People in the group don't want to upset her more by voting against her; on the other hand, if they vote for her it will look to outsiders as if they are happy with what she has said. So after the discussion has gone on for a while, Jake Perry stands up and says, 'I move next business.' If the chair accepts it and someone seconds it, there is an immediate vote without any speeches. Some organizations allow speeches, but only on why you should or should not move on. If the vote is lost, the debate carries on as before. If it's carried, then the meeting goes on immediately to the next item, without discussing the original issue any more. The question hasn't been won or lost; it's been left undecided.

CND used this procedure at the 1984 conference, for instance, to avoid taking a vote on the question of their attitude to the Soviet Union's arms policy.

A third procedural motion is '**previous business**' or '**the previous question**'.

Like the other motions, it can only be proposed by someone who has not already spoken in this debate. According to Citrine, it can also only be taken when an original motion is being discussed, not an amendment. So Mary Dixon might stand up and say, 'I move previous business.' If it is accepted and seconded, there can be a short discussion, but only on this question, not on the main motion. The chair then takes a vote on it. If it is **carried**, the proposer of the original motion replies and the vote is taken. If it is **lost**, there is no right of reply at all, and the meeting goes straight to a vote. So either way it ends discussion.

This is a nastier motion than the others, because whether it's won or lost it stifles the debate. Some organizations do not allow the motion at all. It is the equivalent of taking home the goalposts because you're losing the game.

Sometimes people move 'previous business' thinking that this means they go back to discussing the last item on the agenda. One union's conference recently did this when a decision on pay was taken that the national executive did not like. They went back to their discussion of the item the next day and the executive got the conference to change its mind. Whether the reasons for doing this were good or bad, they were not following the procedure as laid down by Citrine. Constitutionally what they ought to have done was ask for standing orders to be suspended, and then return to the issue and get the motion rescinded (see pp. 48 and 58)

Adjournments

Another way of stopping or postponing a decision is by having an 'adjournment'. You can either adjourn a particular discussion, or the whole meeting. It could be that Jan Marcus brings up an issue which no one really knows much about, so the discussion is going rather vaguely round in circles. Brenda Harbut could say, 'I propose that we adjourn discussion of this issue till next time and that meanwhile Jan goes away and checks the facts.' If the meeting agrees, then the item is on the agenda next time and you can have a proper discussion.

Some sets of standing orders allow you to adjourn a discussion indefinitely. The Latin phrase they use is *sine die* which literally means 'without a day'. The effect is that a date for having another discussion on the issue need not be fixed, so it is in effect dead. This therefore has the same effect as 'next business', but it is less clear what is happening.

You can also have a motion to adjourn the **meeting**, perhaps because it's getting late and most people have left. On p. 22 what would happen if a meeting was adjourned because there was no 'quorum' (that is, not enough people) is explained. If a meeting adjourns for any other reason, it should pick up, on the next occasion, where it left off before. So if you'd got to number 3 out of a list of eight motions, you'd start the next meeting with number 4, and carry on from there.

Some organizations, for instance, Parliament and local councils, have a formal procedure called an 'adjournment motion'. This has a quite different meaning, as it is a device to allow backbenchers, or a minority group, to air their views. They could propose, for instance, 'That this council do now adjourn because of the unsatisfactory nature of the council's policy on privatization.'

The debate will usually be kept short; Wandsworth Council allow two speakers from the opposition and one from the majority party, and then there is a vote. No one expects the motion to be passed, if it were, it would considerably upset the business. But a point of importance to one side will have been raised. You usually have to allow a gap before you can move another adjournment motion – in Wandsworth's case this is an hour – otherwise you could spend the whole time on them and get nowhere with the real business.

Another reason for an adjournment is if a meeting becomes very heated and disorderly. The chair may stop it for a few minutes to allow temperatures to cool; or if two groups could perhaps reach agreement if they were given the chance to discuss a matter privately among themselves. When trade unions are negotiating with management, there may well be frequent adjournments while each side considers its position separately, before coming back for a further discussion.

Reports to meetings

Very often, a substantial part of the time of a general meeting will be taken up with the reports of the executive committee or various subcommittees. On pp. 18–19 the question of who reports to whom, and on what subject, was covered.

A report can be:

- **received for information**. This is when you are hearing about something that has already happened, or hearing from a group whose decisions you have no power to alter. So the planning committee of a council has full powers to decide on planning applications, and its decisions become legally binding as soon as it takes them. Although it tells the council about those decisions in a **report for information**, there's nothing they can do if they don't like them.
- **referred back**. That is, you ask the committee or sub-group to discuss the issue again, because you're not happy with the decision that's been taken.

A typical rule book says:

> A Member who considers that any part of the Annual Report, or of a Standing Orders Committee Report, should not be accepted by the meeting may move its 'reference back' for reconsideration. If seconded, this shall be debated as an amendment to the motion for acceptance of the report. The reference back may include a proposal for amending the part to which objection is made.

In this case, then, you would say, 'I move reference back of Section E for amendment as follows,' and then spell it out. In other cases, for example, the Labour Party, no amendments are allowed.

Some standing orders only allow reference back of certain items. Usually, however, you can refer back all or part of any report.

If you refer back everything, that means you are telling the sub-group to start again from scratch.

If it is a subcommittee or a group which does not have the power to act on its own, then usually the meeting will go through that report item by item, and agree to each. So, for instance, a union branch might have the report of the branch executive in front of it; the chair would say, 'Item 1. Branch support for Haxall's strikers,' and someone might ask a question about it, or might stand up and say, 'I move reference back of the paragraph: "The Branch should be doing more."' This would then be debated and voted on, and other points might also be dealt with in later paragraphs. At the end, the chair ought to say, 'Is that report adopted, except for paragraphs X and Y which have been referred back?' and a vote should be taken. This is often not done; either the chair forgets to go through this stage, or s/he doesn't mention the items that are **not** going to be adopted. This confuses the issue. Have you, by voting for the report as a whole, changed your mind about the reference back? If necessary, ask a question about it before the vote to 'adopt' is taken, even if it means making a nuisance of yourself.

You may also have a report from a **delegate** you have sent to another organization. This could be a simple statement of what happened; for instance, you sent someone to the NCCL annual conference – what were the big issues that were discussed? The formal procedure is for the chair to ask, 'Is that report accepted?' (or 'noted'), but it would be very rare for it not to be; if something has gone wrong, for example, the delegate has not followed policy on a particular issue, it's better to deal with it (because it's easier to see what is happening) by putting a **separate** motion (see pp. 37–42) now, while you are on the subject.

The report might ask you for decisions on various items; perhaps the trades council is organizing a festival and wants to know if its constituent bodies wish to take part. A good delegate makes clear what has to be decided, perhaps by underlining the points in a written report, or stressing them when speaking. The chair must point out each item where a decision is wanted and ask if it's agreed or not.

- Thirdly, a report can be **noted**. This can mean two things. It can be the same as receiving it for **information** (see p. 52). It can also be noted if you don't want to take a decision, or where someone is asking you to agree to something, but you don't want to; 'noting' is a way of turning them down without actually saying so.

So, for example, at your union branch you might have three different items that you 'note'.

First, a report of the CND national conference, given by the delegate from the branch. You listen to him/her, ask questions, and then note it.

Second, a letter from the branch in the next area, telling you about a lobby of Parliament that they're organizing and asking you to join in. Some people in the branch think it's not a very sensible idea, others think that organizing it sounds like a lot of hard work, while others are keen that you should join in. So while some people are proposing that you support the event, someone else says, 'Move we note the letter,' which has the effect that you do nothing, and therefore turn down the idea, without actually saying so.

Another method of achieving the same result is to say that something should 'lie on the table'. This means, again, that no decision is taken. However, while 'noting' something finishes with it, something that is 'lying on the table' can, according to Citrine, be resurrected at future meetings.

The role of the chair

As you can see from all this, the chair has an important place in the standing orders. S/he is there to:

- keep order;
- ensure that people speak at the right point, and in the right way;
- make sure a decision is taken;
- get the meeting to move on to the next item of business at the right time.

The chair therefore has considerable power. On p. 97 some guidelines for chairing sensibly are suggested, so if you are taking on the role of chair, look at these.

Keeping order

This is regarded as very important by Citrine and his followers. Obviously, it does matter that everyone knows what is going on and that only one person is speaking at a time so that you can all hear what s/he is saying. The larger the meeting, the more important this will be. There are several rules which lay down how this is to be done.

The first is that you speak 'through the chair'. A Labour Party guide on meetings (see Further Reading p. 210) has a little cartoon of someone kneeling down to talk through the bars of a chair, but this is not what it means! The idea is that you talk not to the person whose comments you are responding to, but to the chairperson.

The theory behind this is that it stops an argument being personal. To some extent this works in practice, because people have to remember to say 'chair' and this slows them down when otherwise they might be in full flight; it also allows the chair to interrupt to remind them where they are when they are about to punch someone in the face; but it certainly does not prevent some very bitter personal arguments taking place.

Another, better, reason is that having to talk 'through the chair' means that you remember you are talking to the whole meeting, not just one or two people. It is quite difficult for any of us to talk to a large group of people at once; we prefer naturally to deal with only two or three. So it can be useful to have a constant reminder that you are talking not just to your mate Jo, but to Jo and eight other people, six of whom you don't know very well.

Another phrase meaning the same thing that the chair may use is 'all remarks must be addressed to the chair'.

It is usual practice that only one person should talk at a time to the meeting and that people should not chat among themselves while someone is speaking. It is very distracting for the person who is talking if there are other people talking at the same time as you, and it makes it very difficult to hear what's happening.

The chair ought to stop people muttering at the back when one person is talking. Phrases that are often used for this are: 'No private conversations, please'; or 'Can we have some order, please?'; or 'Can we have one meeting?' which are all intended to shut them up.

The rules about interrupting people while speaking are covered on p. 43. Shouting comments (usually rude) from the floor of the meeting is called 'heckling' and can be very difficult for a speaker to cope with, especially if s/he is not very experienced at public speaking. The chair should start by asking these people to shut up. If they go on causing trouble, many standing orders have a procedure called 'naming' the member, which is lifted direct from Parliament.

A typical rule book says:

> Should the Chairman stand while a member is speaking, the member shall immediately cease and resume his seat, and neither he nor any other member shall speak until the Chairman gives leave. For disorderly conduct and refusal to obey the Chair a member may be named by the Chair and removed from the meeting.

Thus 'naming' someone means getting rid of them. It could also be called suspension of the member. This is a point where knowledge of the legal position may be useful, so look at Chapter 10.

Rulings

At a number of points in a meeting the chair must take a decision on what to do. For instance, s/he will need to say whether a point of order (see p. 43) is correct or not, and whether a procedural motion (see p. 48) is accepted or not.

When the chair takes a formal decision about the conduct of the meeting, this is called a ruling. Sometimes what the chair says is final and cannot be challenged. More often, however, there is a procedure for challenging. This could involve:

- one person saying, 'I wish to challenge that ruling,' to start the process; or
- s/he might need to be **seconded** before any action is taken; or
- there might need to be a specific number of people joining in a challenge all at once.

One constitution says:

> The Chair's ruling on any point shall be binding unless it is challenged by any five members. In this event the Chair shall briefly explain the reasons for the decision and then at once put the matter to the vote.

■ Philippa Carr proposes an amendment to a motion that was before the meeting. The chair rules it out of order, on the basis that it was not relevant to the motion. Philippa objects to this, and **challenges** the chair.

In some sets of rules she would be allowed to explain why, but in most cases all she would be allowed to do at this stage is say, 'I challenge the chair's ruling.' The chair should then say, 'Is that supported by four other members?' (The number required will vary between different organizations.) The secretary or vice-chair will then temporarily take over the chair. This may involve them physically changing places, or the secretary may simply take control. Then Philippa states her case and the meeting votes. Citrine says that you need a majority of two-thirds of those voting before this motion to overrule the chair is carried, and organizations generally follow this. (The question of majorities is discussed on p. 23.)

The process is thus often heavily loaded in favour of the chair. Partly this is in order to reduce the chances of someone making a nuisance of himself/herself by challenging all the time; but it also helps to build up the chair's power and authority. If you challenge the chair's ruling, and win, the ruling you want is carried out, but the chair remains in office. If you wish to remove the chair altogether, you would have to move a different motion: 'That this meeting has no confidence in the chair.'

Again, the secretary or vice-chair should take over the chair. The idea behind this is that the chair could not be impartial in controlling a discussion about his/her own case. The person moving the motion is allowed to give the reasons for it, and then the chair replies. The meeting should then vote. You need a two-thirds majority to win. If the vote is passed, then Citrine says that 'the Chairman [*sic*] has no choice but to resign'. Sometimes chairs refuse to accept this. If so, waving Citrine might actually be useful!

If this doesn't work, alternatives are:

- passing a specific motion saying, 'This meeting requires XX to resign from the chair'; or
- abandoning the meeting, and walking out leaving the chair behind. It could then re-start elsewhere with a new person in the chair. If this sort of thing was happening, though, it is likely that the meeting would have effectively dissolved in uproar already.

There is another procedural motion (see p. 48): 'That the chair leave the chair.' Technically, this is another way of adjourning the meeting. If it is passed, the meeting is immediately closed. This is confusing, because people can think it means changing the chair. If someone proposes this, the chair ought to make sure they know what the effect is, before taking it any further.

At the end of the meeting

Standing orders often tell you how long the meeting can be; when it should start, provided enough people are there to make up a quorum (see p. 22 for an explanation of this); when it should end; and what happens to issues you haven't yet raised. For instance, one local Labour Party lays down that the meeting starts at 7.30 p.m. and finishes at 10 p.m. Any business left over is not dealt with. Other ways it could be dealt with are:

- It could be assumed that all the recommendations not discussed are agreed. Confusingly, both this method and the one above can be called the 'guillotine', so if someone uses this word you need to check what they mean; or
- The business left over is 'adjourned' to the next meeting (see p. 51). This can eventually cause chaos. As each meeting overruns, you adjourn more and more business to the next one, so you can end up always one meeting behind; therefore you need to be careful about letting this happen.

- Business not covered is 'remitted' to the executive committee, or some other group. This means it is handed over to them to deal with; since it has not been voted on, they cannot assume it would have been passed, but they can do some further work on the issue and report later to another meeting in order to get a decision.

  Getting items 'remitted' is also sometimes used by those running an organization as a method of avoiding decisions, especially at conferences. See Chapter 7 for more on this.

Suspending standing orders

The standing orders sometimes become difficult to administer, so there is usually a rule allowing you to get past them if necessary. It is made fairly difficult and almost always you need a two-thirds majority to be passed, so that people cannot override the ordinary procedure all the time.

One of the most common reasons for suspending standing orders is that you are running out of time and still have things you want to discuss. For instance, one local Labour Party's standing orders say its meetings end at 10 p.m. They never manage to get through everything by then, as people talk so much, so at every meeting, just before 10 p.m., someone says, 'I move suspension of standing orders'. The chair then asks, 'For how long?' Someone may think the remaining items are going to take 20 minutes, and says so. Someone else wants to go to the pub, and so says 10 minutes instead. There may be a debate about it, but usually there is not, as it would use up even more time. The chair then takes a vote, which requires a two-thirds majority to get through. The logical way to deal with the question is to ask people to vote about carrying on for the longer time (20 minutes) first. If that isn't passed, the chair asks for a vote on 10 minutes. If that doesn't get passed either, then standing orders aren't suspended, and the meeting finishes.

Technically, you should only ask for the particular standing order which deals with this question to be suspended. If you are removing all of them, then logically you don't have a chair or any procedure for running the meeting. People usually ignore this quibble, but it could matter if you are in the middle of a wrangle about something important.

Other reasons for suspending standing orders could be: to allow someone to go on speaking for a longer time than is laid down in the rules; to let someone who is not a delegate, perhaps a visitor from another branch, speak; to let you discuss again something that has already been covered.

Any of the other standing orders could also be suspended; but you always need a two-thirds majority.

There are cases, for example, the Civil and Public Servants Association (CPSA) conference, where **only** the chair can propose the suspension of standing orders. Such examples are rare, but it is worth checking if it applies in your case.

There is also usually a rule about **changing** the standing orders for good. Normally, this involves a two-thirds majority and can only be done at the annual general meeting.

The role of the secretary

Standing orders also tell you what the secretary should do. This job, however, unlike that of the chair, may be divided up among different people; there could for instance be a minutes secretary, a correspondence secretary and a membership secretary.

The essential secretarial work that has to be done, however, whether by one person or three, is:

- making a note of who is at the meeting and who has apologized for not being there;
- keeping 'minutes', that is, the notes of what happens and what decisions are taken (there are details about these on pp. 111–16);
- reporting on letters and reports that have been received, answering them, and following them up between the meetings (see pp. 116–17).

The standing orders do not usually give the secretary a role in conducting the meeting – that is the chair's job – but, in practice, the chair will usually consult him/her over any difficult ruling, or where a problem has arisen. S/he may, however, have to take over the chair if there is decision in which the chair is involved, for instance, on a challenge to a ruling (see above, p. 56).

Checklist

Having read this chapter, you may find it helpful to go through your rule book, or standing orders, or think about the way your group operates, and find the answers to these questions.

clause in
your rules

What sort of meetings do the standing orders apply to (for instance, a branch meeting, a conference, an annual meeting)? (p. 36) ______
What time must the meeting start? (p. 37) ______
Where must it be held? (p. 37) ______
Must people stand up when speaking to the meeting? (p. 42) ______
How are interruptions dealt with? (p. 43) ______
What happens if someone raises a point of order? (p. 43) ______
How do you put forward a motion? (p. 37) ______
How do you put forward an amendment? (p. 40) ______
Is the procedure different for emergency motions? (p. 39) ______
    If so, how? ______
How much notice do you have to give of a motion? (p. 39) ______
Do you need a seconder for a motion or amendment? (p. 40) ______
What's the procedure for voting? (p. 46) ______
Who counts the votes? (p. 47) ______
Is the proposer of a motion allowed to accept amendments? (p. 42) ______
    If not, how does the meeting deal with it? (p. 42) ______
Are there limits on how long you can speak? (p. 42) ______
What procedural motions are allowed? (pp. 48–51) ______
Do they include:
    adjournment (p. 51) ______
    next business (p. 49) ______
    previous business (p. 50) ______
    that the question be put? (p. 49) ______
What subcommittees are there? (p. 52) ______
    How do they report to the main body? (p. 52) ______
How can a ruling by the chair be challenged? (p. 56) ______
How do you suspend standing orders? (p. 58) ______
Can any member move suspension, or must it be the chair? (p. 59) ______

3.

Alternative standing orders

The last chapter explained the procedures by which meetings are conventionally run. These conventional procedures have been built up through long tradition in the labour movement, but they have several disadvantages.

It can be hard to understand what is going on, which makes taking part all the more difficult. This means that power and control are kept in the hands of those who do understand.

People who may be very valuable recruits to the cause can come to these meetings and be entirely put off by the way they are run, so that they may well go away again for good.

These procedures can also make for a very boring evening, except for those few people actually involved in them, such as the officers and those with long experience. In a meeting of 20 or 30 people, perhaps five or six have tasks. The rest are expected to be a passive audience.

The aim of the last chapter was to explain what goes on, so that if you are involved with a group that is run in this way you will know what is happening. But this will not make the meetings themselves any less boring or off-putting. This chapter, therefore, looks at an alternative structure of standing orders.

Often, you will not have a choice about which standing orders you adopt, because they will be dictated to you by the national organization of which your group is just a part. Chapter 4 suggests ways in which, within the formal structure, a meeting can be run more effectively.

This chapter, however, looks at the possibilities when you have a choice about the structure, perhaps because you are setting up a new campaigning group.

Are standing orders needed?

One common reaction after having had bad experiences of formal meetings is for people to say that they don't need any structure at all. There are groups that operate very well like this. Many Greenham

Women's support groups, and the Greenham Common women themselves, for instance, do without a chair, standing orders, procedures of any sort. But there are only a limited number of groups that can work in this way for very long. To do so, people need to:

- have a clear, perhaps fairly limited, aim and function for the group, such as organizing the next outing in support of Greenham Common;
- have a strong commitment to working in a way that does not involve a hierarchy or a structure, but is concerned with co-operation and equality.

Groups like this are hard work and people tend to fall into certain roles. One person may find himself/herself saying several times in the evening, 'Who's going to carry out the decision, then?' while another is constantly trying to pull the discussion back to what is relevant. They are also depressingly easy to disrupt. One person who doesn't share the aims and commitment, but is quite willing to dominate, for instance, can reduce everyone else to tongue-tied silence, afraid to take them on for fear of being put down.

Sometimes you get groups where someone has taken over and, while it's said there is no structure, in fact there are one or two people manipulating the rest. They will have imposed a 'hidden' structure every bit as limiting as the formal one.

If your group can work without a formal structure, well and good. If it can't, what does it need?

In Chapter 1 it was suggested that the needs of most groups were to know who was entitled to come to meetings; when and how they were held; what was to be decided; how the decisions were to be taken; and who was to carry them out.

You may feel that putting all of the 'basic' needs together doesn't leave you with much that's different from the conventional style of meeting. In one way you'd be right, because they are very like the agendas, minutes, resolutions and reports described earlier in this book. Is it going to be possible to break away from them at all?

The reason they do look similar is that underneath the pompous traditions, and the bits and pieces taken over from Parliament, there are some sensible ideas. The basic framework is one that more or less has to exist once you get together a group of more than four or five people. It's the traditions and conventions that rob this framework of common sense and make the meetings tedious.

Is it possible, or reasonable, then, to get rid of the traditions? Perhaps if we're accepting that there has to be a framework, we should accept them too?

But these traditions have been built up for reasons other than simply organizing meetings efficiently – and this is why they often get in the way of decision-making, not help it.

Most of us have been to meetings where only the chair and secretary knew what was going on, and no one else was clear what had been decided, or why. As a result, only the things that the chair and secretary think should occur do occur, and no one else is in a position to protest. That sort of experience is the key to what the traditions are about – power.

A conventionally run meeting is arranged so that a few people are in control, and this gives them power over everyone else. The chair has a little hammer, or a bell, and when s/he rings it, everyone else is supposed to be quiet. Citrine (see p. 37) actually says at one point: 'A Chairman [*sic*] without a bell is like a policeman without a whistle'; this sums up his attitude quite well. The chair lets people speak, or not speak, and decides what is to be discussed, for how long, and in what way. The secretary controls the information coming into and going out of the meeting. A group of others, who 'know the ropes', may also be able to dominate the meeting from among the ordinary members, because they understand the process going on and can turn it to their own advantage.

The rest of the group, meanwhile, sit quietly, perhaps contributing occasionally, but usually willing to let others control what's going on. Often this is not as they would wish – they may want to join in, but find it impossible to make their way into the charmed circle. Or they may not want to talk themselves, but wish others would shut up. Anyone who decides to become involved has got to break in among those in control, in a particular way and at a particular time, and this is difficult.

Running things differently, then, is about changing the way meetings are controlled. It involves shifting the knowledge, and the power, from a small 'leadership' to the group as a whole. This is not easy and it will usually be resisted by those who have the power at the moment, because they are going to lose it. Changing an existing organization is an exhausting task. Setting up a new one that runs in a different way is simpler, but even here you will find people who have operated for so long in the traditional way that they can't believe that any other is possible.

Groups in the women's movement, in peace campaigns and in many community organizations have shown that other approaches **are** possible. And if labour movement organizations don't change, they will find that those who've been active in other organizations, and whom they want to attract, won't come to their meetings because they feel the way of operating is foreign to them.

Greater involvement

The two guiding principles behind any change should be to make sure that everyone can be involved and everyone knows what's happening. This means that the work, and the opportunities for talking, have got to be spread as widely as possible and that the atmosphere is encouraging to those who want to talk. So you need a structure that allows for rotating jobs, creating situations where everyone is expected to participate, and to eliminate anything that will frighten people off. All this needs to be done in a friendly and informal way, if it is not to be intimidating.

Bearing this in mind, the next sections work through the various possibilities. At the end, there is an example of a 'model' set of standing orders, covering the important points, which you can use or adapt for your group. They are intended to apply to smallish groups – rather than tiny ones of three or four people which can manage without any real structure or big conferences; the latter are considered in Chapter 7. Read this chapter in conjunction with Chapter 5, which looks at how a meeting actually runs in practice.

It is very important that the 'officers' are not a small exclusive group with all the power, even if they are willing to exercise it in a friendly way. It's therefore essential to spread the jobs so that far more people get to do something. This can happen in two ways:

- You could split the responsibilities into small manageable chunks, so that most people have something to do. One person could take notes of the meetings; another could deal with the letters; a third could look after the membership records.
- Alternatively, you could **rotate** the jobs, so that different people do them at different meetings or for a month at a time. This is very good for spreading the power, but it can lead to hitches when information doesn't get passed on, or when this month's secretary or chair is ineffective.

You can do different things with different jobs. It is probably necessary to have a permanent **treasurer**, who is confident with money and trustworthy. If you have a bank account, the bank will need to know who can sign cheques, and you cannot change that person every month. The **contact address** for the group also needs to be permanent. If you want to make it easy for new people to join, they have got to know where to find you. If one person acts as a contact address, however, this does not mean they have to do all the work arising from this themselves. New members' enquiries, for instance, could be passed to the person currently holding the membership file.

So the group needs to work out:

- what jobs need to be done regularly; and
- how you are going to organize them.

If you have fixed jobs, how long are they going to last? It could be six months, a year, two years. When are you going to decide about changes? The most usual way is to have a bigger meeting once a year.

If you are rotating the jobs, how will you know who has which job this time? This is particularly a problem if you have a different chair at each meeting, because you have to decide whose turn it is each week or month. Meetings can waste time while some people avoid volunteering in case they are thought too pushy and shy people sit hoping not to be noticed, until finally someone is pressganged into the job. There are two possible ways of dealing with this:

- Decide who is taking the chair for the next meeting at the end of the previous one. People should have become more relaxed and therefore more willing to volunteer by then. The person who's agreed has a responsibility to persuade someone else, if for some reason s/he needs to drop out at the last minute.
- Have a rule, however silly or arbitrary, that you obey, which makes sure that everyone has a turn. It could be by age, by alphabetical order, by the order on the membership list. Decide on the rule, and stick to it. If the next person on the list isn't there, go on to the one after that. If you do this, no one will feel picked upon or that there is a popularity poll going on.

You can use the same method for the other jobs, such as the secretary; or you could say that whoever is chair this month is secretary next, membership secretary the one after, so that the jobs pass gradually down a line of people.

Members

The problem for most groups is having too few people come, not in restricting the numbers! However, the question of who's entitled to be there can cause difficulties, especially if a controversial decision has been taken.

In a formal group, there's no problem. People will be members because they have paid a subscription; and they will probably have a membership card. The committee will have been elected and be a fixed number. If 'observers' are allowed, they won't be permitted to vote when decisions are made.

Groups running on a less formal model usually try to operate without a committee, as explained on pp. 61–2, and also without a tight membership list, so that anyone interested is allowed to come along. In theory, this should make the discussion more democratic and more relevant. The drawbacks are, however, that:

- different groups of people may come to successive meetings, so that you have to spend time going over the same ground, repeating the discussion you had last time, and perhaps reversing your decision, to the confusion of everyone;
- a small group may be able to turn up and hijack the meeting, manipulating the organization in a particular direction; or
- since everyone can turn up, no one does, because they assume someone else is doing all that is necessary.

You cannot entirely avoid these dangers in an informal group, unless everyone is committed enough to turn up regularly. However, if there is a concentrated administrative task to be done, perhaps organizing a conference, you may need to hand it over to a smaller group that has a fixed membership, and let them go away and get on with it. Either lay down **policy** in advance, or ask them to come back with proposals for that policy; but let them deal with the 'nuts and bolts' without interference, reporting back to you afterwards.

You may not be able to do without a permanent committee, however, if your organization is large and shapeless, with many people coming and going.

■ Edward's community centre has a lunch club, an after-school club and half a dozen evening classes. Everyone who comes to these becomes a member of the Community Association, but for most their involvement is very limited, and they certainly don't want to get involved in the management of the centre. So the association has to have a committee of the people most involved to get the work done at all, although they agree that anyone else can come along and take part in the discussion. They have decided to avoid voting and work by **consensus** (see p. 70). So it doesn't usually matter whether people are on the committee or not. When they do come to a vote, though, they have agreed that only the members can vote.

Finding out about the meeting

People must know when the meeting is if they are to come. This can be a problem with a less formally organized group. People often fix the date of the next meeting at the end of the last, so that you only know when it is if you were there. The others all need to be told, far enough in advance to be able to make their arrangements for childcare or transport. Not having sufficient notice is one of the ways in which everyone except young, mobile people with cars are excluded from a group. So you need to say that people must be told about the next meeting, perhaps a week in advance.

What about people who very rarely come to meetings, but who want to be kept in touch, and with whom you want to keep in touch? CND suggest (see Further Reading, on p. 210) that you add up the number of people who are members 'on paper' and divide them by the number who come to meetings. Then each of the regular attenders takes the responsibility of talking to some of them, both to tell them what's going on and to find out what their feelings are, between meetings.

In the Labour Party, to take another example, there are 'collectors' who are supposed to do this job as they pick up subscriptions or deliver the ward newsletters; but often they don't, partly because they are each given too much work. If you spread the task out, and give everyone a few people to call on, those involved are less liable to feel put upon and the job becomes more manageable. Inevitably, some members will promise to do their share and then not carry it out, but if this is just a few people it will not matter too much.

Where and when to hold the meetings is dealt with in Chapter 4. The chapter also suggests you should pay childcare expenses or arrange a childcare rota, and organize giving lifts. If you're drawing up standing orders, include these points, because this means there is no argument about people's entitlement, and people can see that their rights are clearly written down and so will feel less embarrassed about asking for them.

What are you going to discuss?

A formal meeting will have an 'agenda' (see p. 99) which lists what you are going to discuss. A list of some sort is needed at any meeting, so that you can sort out what needs to be dealt with and when something's going to come up. It also helps the group allocate its time properly, so that enough is left for the more important items.

Traditionally, the secretary draws up the agenda in advance, discussing it with the chair. For a big meeting, this may be the best way to do it. An alternative, however, is to start the meeting by asking people what needs to be dealt with, and writing this down.

Even if the agenda is drawn up in advance, some groups spend the first five minutes 'reviewing' it, that is, checking over what is on it and confirming that it is correct. Perhaps something can't be discussed yet, because something else hasn't happened, so you can remove it from your list before you start.

You may wish to set a rough timetable, and the person chairing could suggest, for instance, 'Let's spend an hour on the main question, and move on to other matters not later than nine o'clock.' If people have agreed this at the beginning, they are less likely to protest later.

It is the role of the person taking the chair to ensure:

- that the meeting keeps more or less to this timetable;
- that the discussion remains relevant;
- that anyone who wants to participate in the discussion gets a chance to do so;
- that a decision is reached at the end.

However, if something is important, perhaps because it involves spending a lot of money, or is controversial, or affects a particular member or a small group more than others, or affects the staff, then people do have a right to know in advance that it is coming up. Perhaps they will need to make special arrangements to ensure they can get there, and they might need to do some extra homework, looking up facts or thinking where they stand on a particular issue. If you took a decision, for example, to sell your building, without telling people it was coming up, it would almost certainly be overturned if it came to court (see Chapter 10).

Tell people in advance, therefore, about the items you know have got to be covered and then write the complete agenda at the meeting, so that it is up to date.

Say in your standing orders that you won't take any big decisions, except in an emergency, without having warned people in advance about them.

Proposals

If you are taking complicated or important decisions, it is **essential** that people know what you are discussing, what they are voting on and what you have decided; this may mean being more formal than you would like at times.

The points on which you have to decide have to be summed up, so that people can say whether they are **for** or **against** them. This could be called a **proposal**, a **motion** or a **resolution**. In the rest of this section it is called a **proposal**.

Formal sets of rules also quite often say that proposals have to be circulated in advance (see p. 39). This has the advantage that people know what is being discussed and can decide whether they are interested enough to come along. On the other hand, it means that you cannot shape your decision around what you have discovered during the discussion.

An alternative method is to lay down that you will say in advance that you are going to have a discussion on, say, running a new campaign, out of which you hope a proposal will come. Then people who are interested in the subject will know that they should come, you can have the discussion, and different ideas can be floated, before you finally come up with something that is agreed by all of you, or at least a majority.

Use a blackboard or large sheets of paper to write down the proposal, and any alterations that are suggested as they arise, so that people can have an idea of what is being put forward in front of them. If you make the proposers do the writing, it may discourage them from being verbose!

The formal process that is described on p. 40 has been overlaid by a great deal of verbiage, but the bare bones are common sense. These are that:

- one person puts forward an idea;
- the chair checks that there is at least some support for it by asking for a 'seconder' before you spend too much time discussing it – though for a small group, you might not wish to bother with this;
- people who think the proposal is on the right lines but could be improved suggest alterations;
- you discuss the issue and the suggested alterations;
- you decide first on the alterations and **then** on whether the proposal itself is the right one.

Decisions

In formal meetings, the method of deciding on something is usually to vote, and this procedure is often gone through even when it's clear that everyone agrees. Other groups, however, try to operate more by way of a **consensus**. This is a Latin word meaning consent and it means that you talk something through until either an agreement is reached, or those who object are willing to drop their opposition for the sake of the group. This can take much longer, but it will result in a more united and committed group in the end. You may want to decide, therefore, that you will operate by consensus wherever you can.

However, it is not sensible to say that you will never have votes, because:

- on trivial matters, there's no point in carrying on arguing about something people are not too bothered about anyway. If you've decided to have cups of tea at the next meeting, and someone suggests you have coffee, if you can't have both it's not worth having a long discussion. Just vote, and find out which the majority prefer. This is often called having a 'straw poll' or a 'sense vote', to emphasize that it is not a matter of principle, simply a way of testing feelings.
- on points where there is a real split within the group that no amount of discussion is going to heal and there is no possible compromise, carrying on arguing is not going to solve anything and might destroy the goodwill in the group. So after you've thrashed out all the points, you may need to take a vote.

■ Mary Ellis's group are thinking of applying for a grant from the council to do their club room up. Two people object because the council may attach conditions to the grant. After discussing the issue for a while, neither side is convinced by the other's arguments, so they have to vote on it, and the two who disagree are overruled.

In this example, to reach agreement all round is impossible, but to drop the matter because you couldn't get agreement would mean that the majority gave way to the minority, which is not logical. Only trial and error can tell you when a vote is needed and when it is not. Use common sense rather than a rule book. If your group has decided that it will usually run by consensus, the chair should ask, 'Do people agree that we need to vote on this?' before actually doing so.

Avoiding decisions

There are many occasions, however, when it is not sensible to take a decision. You may realize that you do not have enough information, or else none of the ideas that have been put forward turn out to be satisfactory. So at times you will want to agree:

- to postpone the matter until next time – because you don't have the facts, or because the individual concerned is not present. When you do this, try to make a rule that at the same time you decide **who** is going to find out the facts, or persuade the person concerned to come. Don't just leave it, or you still won't be able to get anywhere next time.

- to drop the matter. This could happen when you feel you've discussed it enough and can get no further. In the example on p. 70, reaching a definite decision would simply create too much of a problem. Another case might be a question you originally thought it was right for the group to deal with, but now realize is beyond your powers. For example, the Gateway Community Centre committee are asked to support an appeal by NALGO against the deportation of one of their members. They are very sympathetic, but know that they do not really have a role, and are afraid that the council will hold it against them if they take a 'political' stand and perhaps stop their grant aid. So rather than reject the appeal, they decide to drop the matter.

Moving on

Quite often, an item is discussed for longer than it needs to be, when people are in fact agreed on a course of action but no one is quite sure how to bring the talking to an end. You also need to agree, therefore, that a proposal 'to come to a decision' can be taken. If others support it, then the chair should sum up, establish the meeting's view, and move on.

Try to avoid having a long discussion on questions about whether to take a decision, or whether to drop or hold over a question. This should stop people getting bogged down in questions about how the meeting is operating, rather than the issues themselves. You may want to limit the number of people who speak for and against these proposals, perhaps to two on each side. However, rely on common sense, rather than hard rules – there are cases where it will be necessary to have a longer discussion.

You may also want to vote fairly quickly on these issues, even if you normally try to work by consensus.

Who does what?

Deciding on the issue itself is only half the business. The other half is to decide who is carrying it out. If your decision is simply a question of policy – for instance, 'are we for or against the sale of council houses?' – there is nothing else to decide. As soon as you start wanting to tell people your views, or want to take action because of them, someone has got to be responsible. They won't just happen. So have a pretty firm rule that you never move on until you've agreed what happens next.

You cannot rely on the chair and the secretary to bail you out, as a formal meeting does (although in practice they are often very bad at it). So establish:

- that every decision is to include agreement about **who** is doing it;
- that at the beginning of the next meeting you will go through and check that it has been done.

■ Howard's meeting agrees they are against the sale of council houses. Darren agrees to write to the leader of the Labour Party on the council to say so. Josie will issue a press release about it. At the next meeting, when they are going through the notes of this one, the person in the chair says, 'Have the press release and letter been sent out?' If not, the meeting will have to discuss whether it is now too late, or can the situation be rescued?

Sub-groups and working parties

Often, having decided something, putting it into effect turns out to mean more work than one person can do, or there might be a need for detailed discussion on a particular point.

For instance, Celia's Women's Project is putting in grant applications to three different organizations. They decide that the only way to handle it is to split into three groups, one to concentrate on each application.

To stop the project fragmenting, however, any sub-group that is set up needs to know precisely what work it has to do; by what date; whom it's got to report to or liaise with; and what powers it has.

So the Women's Project sub-groups must know whether they are actually to send off the grant applications, or just to prepare them for the group as a whole to approve, and, if the latter, which meeting they will have to get them ready for. If they are reporting back with recommendations, they will probably find it very annoying if these are ignored and the whole thing discussed a second time. Handing out work to sub-groups is only really useful if they are given responsibility to get on with the job. If they aren't, it won't even save you time in the long run and it will put people in a bad temper.

On other occasions, you might want a group to do some research for you and to come up with a range of options. Provided they know that this is all they are being asked to do, it can be very useful.

■ Shabir's union branch do not feel they know enough about the National Council for Civil Liberties to agree to affiliate or not. So they ask three people to find out about it, and present the arguments for and against at the next meeting, when they will decide. The three people, therefore, go off to find out about NCCL, their union head office's policy towards it and whether there is a local group they can link up with; then they report this back to everyone else.

If your group is large, you might wish to have permanent sub-groups dealing with special subjects. You might have one group dealing with social events and another with planning your next conference, for instance. There is a danger that you may become bureaucratic and your time may be taken up with reports from other groups and wrangles about what was decided. One possible way to reduce the chance of this is to make sure that everyone knows when the sub-group meetings are held, and allow anyone who wishes to go along to do so. This means that it is difficult to raise suspicions afterwards about any 'funny business' or to suggest that the sub-group is getting remote. You can always say, 'Well, you had the chance to go along.' Another possibility is to rotate the membership of the groups in the same way as you do the officers. Perhaps a different three people each month, or each quarter, could be responsible for looking after the building, for example. The drawback of this is that if the group has been set up because it is a specialist area, or because only a few people are really interested in it, rotating the tasks will mean they are not done well.

Often, the notes of the meetings of smaller groups are sent out to everyone for information. This can be expensive on postage but it is helpful. The person chairing the meetings of the main group will then have to ensure that familiar points are not discussed over and over again.

The thing to avoid, if at all possible, is a special 'executive' who take key decisions and are separate from, and therefore more knowledgeable than, anyone else. If you are splitting the work between groups, try to make sure that everyone is involved in one. Inevitably, some people will have more time, and more energy, than others, but at least people should all have the **chance** to be equally involved.

If you have regular general meetings, sub-groups should be asked to report to them directly.

Difficult people

It is harder for an informal group to deal with someone who wants to make life difficult for the rest of you than it is for a formal group. At least under the formal procedure the chair has methods to force them to leave the meeting (see p. 55). An informal group has to rely much more on collective pressure and the weight of collective disapproval.

Here are some suggestions:

- If someone is talking too much and trying to monopolize the meeting, the chair is entitled to say, 'Now you've had your turn, would you like to give X or Y a chance?' and others can then back this up.
- If someone is being unpleasant to others, the chair can ask them to desist, and also do something that tends to disarm them, that is, ask them why they are behaving in this way. Is someone, or something annoying them?
- If there is someone who is not supposed to be there – a man in a women-only meeting, for instance – you can start by appealing to him and explaining why he is not wanted, and then, if necessary, simply ignore him totally or, if that is too difficult, move to another room. However, you may find that you have to give up and bring the meeting together again another time. It is sensible, though, only to do this after a vote by the rest of the meeting to exclude the offender. This should happen even if your meeting does not usually take votes, just in case of a further challenge later, perhaps even in the courts.

Closing a meeting

One problem with a non-formal meeting is that it can drag on. People are so anxious not to seem to put pressure on each other that they can take too long on each issue. It is useful, therefore, for the group to take a decision about what time they would like their meeting to finish, and to stick to it as closely as possible. After you have been talking as a group for more than two hours or so, people tend to run out of ideas and energy; since nothing very productive will come out of it, you might as well finish.

If there seems to be too much business, one possibility is to confine the meeting to the items on which a *decision* has to be made, and to make the information-giving part – when people report on other groups they have attended, tell you about the benefit disco that is going on next week, and sell you the tickets for the Christmas draw – into a more social event. So you could start at 7.30, work through till 9.30, and either break for coffee and a chat about these items or go to the pub or a café.

However, try to ensure that you always deal with the bureaucratic clearing-up before you break; that is, deal with the date of the next meeting (but see also p. 67); who is chairing and taking notes at it; any jobs that haven't yet been parcelled out.

Some groups also set aside 10 minutes or so at the end to have a brief 'meeting review' where they discuss what went right and what went wrong. How this works in practice is explained on p. 111.

Longer-term policy

You may find that there are larger issues coming up, particularly on long-term policy, than can be dealt with in a regular evening meeting, and that these are constantly being pushed to one side to make way for organization points that can't wait. Some groups arrange to have an occasional long meeting – half a day or all day at a weekend, or even a whole weekend away somewhere. At these, they can deal with issues in a more relaxed way, review where they are and where they should be, and decide on what they are doing next. They may do this when they feel it is necessary, or as policy they may agree it should happen once a year. Balham Family Centre Management Committee, for example, spends a day 'reviewing' itself each year. They bring in a sympathetic outsider, someone they all know and trust but who is not actually on the management committee, to chair it.

Arranging something like this will take extra work, since it will mean arranging a crèche, somewhere to meet, and doing something about lunch and refreshments, but it may be worth it. If you don't feel such a long time is necessary, but that nevertheless policy matters are slipping from your grasp, you could say that you will have an extra meeting at the ordinary time, or set aside one of your ordinary meetings for this, keeping other matters down to a minimum.

Taking notes

This is another job that can be rotated, so that a different person does it at each meeting. Once again, try to develop an arrangement so that people know in advance that it's their turn. You also need to establish that people do not have to bear the cost of postage or photocopying themselves, but that the group will repay them. Some ideas on how you can do this are given on p. 120.

People may feel rather daunted by the idea of taking notes, but it is not that difficult. The important points to get down are what was decided and who is going to carry it out.

It is useful to have enough information in the notes to explain why a particular decision was reached, but not vital. If it was agreed to discuss something at the next meeting, it's important to put that down, as this will help when drawing up the list of points to be discussed.

So, for example, the notes of a group discussion on applying for a grant might read:

> Ellen introduced the discussion on whether we should apply for a grant from the council, and, after explaining the advantages and disadvantages, proposed that we should. Eric and Martha objected, saying they did not wish to be tied to the council's conditions for grants. After a discussion, it was agreed to vote, and the proposal to apply for a grant was accepted by 18 votes to two.
>
> Ellen said she would get the forms from the council and meet Martin before the next meeting to make a list of what needed doing. We agreed to discuss the question again during the May meeting.

If a question is not discussed because there is not enough information (see p. 70) someone must agree to get that information, and this also must appear in the notes. So, at the same meeting, the next point might have been, 'Eric said we might have to obtain planning permission, but it was agreed not to discuss this in detail yet because we did not know the facts. Eric agreed to find out the position and tell us at the next meeting.'

Summary of alternative standing orders

This list is intended only as guidance on the points to consider, rather than to become new tablets of stone in the way Citrine has become. You could decide that when any problem about your procedure arises, you'll follow these guidelines; or you could write your own. Some of the points in here, for example, on suspending standing orders or on challenging the chair's ruling, are discussed in Chapter 2 rather than here, so consult this chapter also.

1. The Group is the XYZ Group. Anyone who lives in the Borough of XYZ is allowed to join the meetings, on payment of the membership fee. However, at committee meetings, only those who have been elected by the members at the Group's Annual General Meeting are allowed to vote. The minimum number ('quorum') for a general meeting is 20, and for a committee meeting is four committee members.
2. The Group will have a general meeting once a quarter and a committee meeting once a month. All members will be notified at least seven days in advance of the general meeting and committee members will be notified at least seven days in advance about committee meetings. The Group will bear the cost of childcare

incurred by members attending their meetings, to a maximum of £X a meeting.

3. The Committee will consist of 10 people, to be elected by secret vote at the Annual General Meeting each year. The tasks of chairing the meetings, keeping the notes, answering the letters and keeping the membership records up to date will rotate among the committee members, each month, taking the members in alphabetical order. The person carrying out any task in one month is responsible for passing on the papers to the person carrying it out in the next month.

4. The person whose job it is to chair, and the person who will be keeping the notes, will agree a draft list of items for discussion each month, for circulation beforehand. Anyone who wants to put something on that list should contact one of them. At the beginning of the meeting the draft list ('agenda') will be agreed by those present, with anything necessary being added or subtracted. The person in the chair will then put forward a rough timetable for the meeting's agreement, and the group will then try to stick to this.

5. The person taking the notes ('minutes') should try to write down a summary of the discussion, a note of the decisions made, and the name of the person(s) asked to carry out the decision. This person should then type, or write up neatly, these notes and circulate them together with the agenda for the next meeting to the other Committee members at least a week beforehand. The Group will pay any reasonable postage and photocopying costs incurred in doing this.

6. The person taking the chair is responsible for keeping order, for keeping discussion to relevant points, and for moving on to the next item at the appropriate time.

7. Decisions will generally be taken by consensus, unless the chair considers that:

(a) it is too minor a matter to spend a long time in discussion;
(b) there is no possibility of agreement; or
(c) it is one of the procedural points listed in para. 8 and a vote is the best way to decide.

8. During any discussion, at a general meeting or Committee meeting, a member may propose:

(a) that a decision is reached with no further discussion;
(b) that the decision is deferred until a later meeting; or
(c) that no decision is taken.

Any of these proposals must be seconded, and will then be briefly discussed and agreement reached, or a vote taken. It is a matter for the chair's judgement whether to have a vote or not.

9. Where the meeting wishes to reach a definite decision on its policy or on a course of action, members will be asked to put forward proposals, that is, short statements summarizing their views. Any proposal put forward should be supported by another person ('seconded') before it is discussed in detail. Any other member is entitled to put forward a proposal to alter the original one (an 'amendment'). An amendment must not be indirect contradiction of the proposal. Proposals or amendments will either be circulated in writing, or put up on the blackboard or poster on the wall, during the discussion.

10. The Committee can appoint sub-groups and working parties as necessary. These will be open to all Committee members and Group members who wish to attend. A report of the reasons for setting up any sub-group, and of its activities, will be given to the general meeting after its setting up. Details of the meetings, and notes of their decisions, will be circulated to all Group members.

11. Before any meeting ends, agreement about who is carrying out any activity decided upon, and who is doing the routine tasks for the next month, must be reached.

12. Meetings should not start before 7.30 p.m., or go on beyond 10 p.m. If there is too much business, or a need to resolve longer-term policy issues, then an occasional weekend meeting will be arranged. At this a crèche will be provided and paid for by the Group.

13. If there is any disagreement with the way the meeting is being chaired, any member can ask for a vote on a particular ruling. To win against the chair, a two-thirds majority of those voting is required.

14. The Group can agree to suspend any of these standing orders, but there must be a vote, and a two-thirds majority is required to win.

15. By agreement of the meeting, an individual can be banned from attendance at either a general meeting or a Committee meeting, if s/he is making it too difficult for the meeting to continue. If there is not a consensus, this requires a two-thirds majority of those present and voting to be effective.

16. These standing orders can be changed by a two-thirds majority of those present at a general meeting, so long as notice of the proposed changes has been given in advance.

4.

Meetings in practice

This chapter looks at the way in which a meeting *actually* happens within the framework of standing orders explored in Chapter 2. The difference is important: a clear set of standing orders is no guarantee that the meeting will run well, even if you follow them to the letter. So this chapter tells you how meetings are usually run and suggests what good practice is. Even if you don't want to adopt all the ideas, it may help you to think about ways of making your meetings better.

The chapter is intended to cover smaller local meetings, like a committee, or a trade-union or Labour Party branch. That is, groups which are bound by a certain amount of procedure and which tend to have routine items coming up month after month. Even if well-organized, these are often rather dull. In the next chapter there are suggestions for making them livelier and for working in a different, less formal way. This chapter, however, covers the conventional ways in which they are organized, and how to help them run smoothly. Chapter 6 covers annual general meetings, and Chapter 7 deals with big conferences.

For any group, of any size, the more preparation you do the better the group will run. If everyone turns up at the last minute, without having thought about anything since the last meeting, you'll be wasting time because promises made to take action won't have been carried out, people won't have thought any more about the policies, and you'll spend half the time waiting while the secretary shuffles the papers. At the very least, **after** each meeting the officers should talk to people who've said they'll do a particular task and then chase them up if they haven't done it. Then, just **before** each meeting, they must make time to think about the agenda, to discuss it between them, to get the correspondence in order and to check on any outstanding points.

If this doesn't happen, and it all seems like too much bother, the time has possibly come to consider whether this particular meeting or set of meetings has a useful role to play at all. Perhaps the group has outlived its usefulness, if no one's sufficiently interested to do anything about it between meetings. If so, you have two alternatives:

scrap it, or give it a new lease of life by altering its role.

You may however not be able to do either, at least formally. It may be fixed in the constitution, so it's got to continue meeting even if no one's interested. You might be able to think of some way, even so, to improve it. For instance, could you have a very short formal branch meeting, followed by the showing of a video and a discussion?

Before you get to that stage, however, think about the preparations you make and how welcoming you are to new people or shy people.

Place and time

This is often laid down in the rule book, but for an established group it may be a matter of custom going back over a number of years. For a new group just starting up, or one that's taking on a new life, there are several points you should take into account before deciding on a meeting place and time.

Place

How easy is the place for people to get to and how welcome will they feel when they get there?

- A gloomy hall in a dimly lit back street, or a union office in a deserted shopping precinct, will be offputting to women, elderly people and anyone who's easily frightened.
- A lot of stairs and no lift could prevent people with disabilities, older people, and anyone with a pram, from attending.
- A room in a pub may be offputting, especially for women and people who don't drink, including those from ethnic or religious groups which forbid alcohol. Many Muslims or Baptists, for example, do drink, but those who don't may strongly dislike going to a place where alcohol is served.
- This drawback applies even more strongly to working men's clubs, and in addition some of these still bar women or restrict the rooms they can go into. Some clubs are also racist.
- Going to an individual member's house may embarrass some people, who feel they are intruding on someone else's private life.

So the place you always have met, or the place that is easiest and cheapest to book, may not be the most suitable if you think about it from these various points of view.

Look around for alternatives. Try asking in the local library for a list of halls for hire; ask the school secretary or head teacher about using a local school; or a vicar about using the church hall; or a local community centre, or the offices of a voluntary group, or the library itself.

You may not be able to find a place that is perfect in every way. It may not exist in your area, or be too expensive, or be booked up by others who got there first. Having done the best you can, there are ways of minimizing the disadvantages.

You can organize lifts for people, or at least make sure that people are accompanied to the venue by fellow members. On p. 83 it is suggested that for any meeting, however conventional, the secretary should ask people who need a lift to get in touch. But it may be important to put more effort into it than this and arrange for someone to ring round those who are likely to have difficulties, offer a lift and arrange for someone to provide it. If there are not enough cars to make this possible, then simply offering company, someone to knock on the door and walk down to the meeting place can be a help. One woman going into a pub may find it an ordeal, for instance; two together will feel much less daunted.

Having got people there, make sure that someone also takes responsibility for getting them home again. If the walk was daunting at 7.30 in the evening, it will be even more so at 10.

If the best room you can find is not accessible to the disabled, it's best to say so, with apologies, in any letters that go out. But if you have disabled members who'd like to come – and the only way to find that out is to contact them and ask – you could try asking several people to be ready to lift a wheelchair, or provide whatever help is necessary. Check first, though, that there isn't a second special entrance, marked with a wheelchair sign. Most public halls have these (all of them should have), though it may mean going round by the dustbins and having a door specially unlocked for you.

Time

When is the meeting happening? Any time is going to be difficult for someone, but some times are worse than others for particular groups.

- For people with young children, most times are bad, but between about 4 p.m. and 7 p.m. is worst of all, because they are giving the children their tea, putting them to bed, and so on. 'Straight after work' is impossible for many working parents who may have a makeshift arrangement with someone to look after their child for the couple of hours after school, or may know that s/he is alone in the house and rapidly getting bored and hungry. Theoretically, this drawback should apply to both mothers and fathers. Things being what they are, many fathers don't take their responsibilities seriously, so it is more of a problem for mothers.

- A meeting in working time may be fine for professionals, especially if they can claim some connection with their work, and for retired and unemployed people. Manual workers and clerical workers, however, are likely either to find it impossible to get away, or lose wages if they do.
- Weekends present difficulties for parents, and indeed anyone who goes to work during the week, especially if the meeting starts too early. You cannot get to the shops, change your library books, go to the dry-cleaner's, and get to a meeting, all before 10 a.m. If you must have a meeting which starts that early, then at least it should stop while the shops are still open, so that people can make a dash for them.

You must think about the sort of people you want to come to your meetings, and therefore what time of day is most suitable for your group. It might be necessary to vary the times so that different groups can come. One APEX branch, with members in different workplaces, holds its meetings alternately at 3.30 p.m. and 5.30 p.m., and also rotates round the different workplaces. For the 3.30 meeting, the clerical staff at the particular workplace can come, but some of those at distant locations can't. For the 5.30 meeting, not many women clerical staff can come, but other workers find it easier.

Weekday evenings, starting about 7.30 p.m. and ending about 10 p.m. suit many people. If they end later, people will drift off anyway. But this, and indeed almost any time, does raise the problem of childcare, and the care of other dependants, such as elderly or disabled relatives, as well.

In any group, you should make an effort to arrange childcare, although many people will still find it too complicated to come. Here are some possible ways of organizing this:

- Set up a rota of the branch members who do not have children. If there is another branch that meets on a different night, you could link with them so your members babysit for them and theirs for you, so that no one need miss a meeting. To arrange this, you need to have a list of volunteers and one person to co-ordinate. The co-ordinator could change from time to time – perhaps people could agree to do three-month stints. Anyone who needs a babysitter then rings up the co-ordinator who will find a volunteer. Don't let men who have children volunteer; they ought to be looking after their own children so that their wives can go out.

- Alternatively, or in addition, you can pay childcare expenses. Find out from people in your area who babysit what the 'going rate' is for the job and publicize that you will pay up to that level. It will be important to pay out in a way that doesn't make anyone feel embarrassed about asking for the money. Perhaps a form could be left on every chair, or there could be a question on the 'credential' (see p. 98): 'Do you require babysitting expenses?' For groups that pay delegates' travelling and subsistence expenses, like many union branches, childcare can simply be added on.
- A third possibility, for a larger group, may be arranging a crèche. Details of how to do this are not covered here (look at *Organising Things*, pp. 188–192; see Further Reading on p. 210 for details). A proper crèche takes a lot of work and even so you may not get many children, because it will be too complicated to get them dressed, and all their equipment together, and bring them out; many children object to going to crèches anyway. An exception to this, and one relevant to the time of a meeting, is if you were actually holding it on the premises where the children were cared for during the day anyway, or could persuade those places to stay open later and look after the children longer. Then it would be sensible to have a meeting straight after people finish work and keep the children in their nursery or after-school club a bit longer.

One other possibility is for the children themselves to come to the meeting. This can be pretty boring for them, and if they start playing up or asking to go home their parents may feel they have to leave with them, but it usually does a lot to break down the formalities and makes people more friendly if there are small babies and toddlers around.

If you are in a group that has resisted the idea of making proper childcare arrangements, or has not put any effort into making them work, then for people with childcare responsibilities to bring their children along, perhaps as an organized protest, might emphasize its importance and alter the attitudes of the rest. Think it out carefully, though; other people could make nasty remarks and it is hard on the children.

Telling people about the meeting

The first thing is to let people know that a meeting is happening. This is called **giving notice** of the meeting. How much notice, and in what way, is usually covered in your constitution or standing orders (see p. 21).

Depending on what sort of group you are, you might need to send a letter to people's home addresses, circulate an agenda in the workplace or put up a poster, or do all three.

The notice can be a very short letter, with all the details sent separately, or you can include the details in the notice itself.

Even if it is not laid down in your standing orders, try to give at least a week's notice of meetings, sending the detailed papers at the same time if you can.

Often a habit develops of sending out details about the meeting only just before it is due. Doing the mailing is seen as a chore which is less important than other things. However, if people only hear about the meeting, and what is to be discussed, very late,

- few people will turn up to the meeting because they will not have remembered about it, or will not have been able to arrange a babysitter;
- they will not have read through the papers, so that the discussion is less well informed and more muddled than it needs to be.

Sometimes, however, sending out the papers late is a deliberate way of keeping power in the hands of bureaucrats by making it difficult for others to know what is going on. If there are a lot of papers and they only appear a couple of days before the meeting, you'll be pushed to read them in time. The TUC, for example, sends out an inch-thick pile of documents for its committees to the busy trade-union officials who sit on them three days in advance. Of course this means they will not have time to read them, so on the day of the meeting they have to take on trust what the TUC staff are saying about the papers.

In return for the secretary sending things out in good time, however, the ordinary member has a duty to read the papers properly. Hurriedly scanning a document and then raising a point that actually comes up on the next report, which you haven't read yet, is infuriating for anyone else and suggests you are not taking the meeting seriously enough.

Organizations develop a style over the years in what they send out to their members in advance of meetings. Some have only a half-sheet of paper, some a great parcel. There's no set rule, and a new secretary might want to look at what his/her organization is doing and see if something should be changed. Usually there will be some or all of these: the notice of the meeting; the 'agenda'; the 'minutes' of the last meeting; any resolutions; any reports that are going to be discussed.

The notice

This is often in the form of a letter, which does not vary much from meeting to meeting, and can be full of pompous phrases like 'I hereby give you notice' or 'Notice is hereby given'. These are offputting and quite unnecessary; what they need to say is, 'There is a meeting at . . . on . . . and all members have the right to come along', in as simple a way as possible.

It should say when and where the meeting is. If it's awkward to get there, or if it is a new venue, it should say how to get there. Try to tell people if you can arrange lifts or childminding, and if there is disabled access.

■ Tony sends out the letter for the October branch meeting saying:

Dear Member,
The next meeting of the Cleobury Branch is on Thursday 12 October at Old Street Meeting Hall at 8 p.m. The hall is at the corner of Old Street and New Alley, and the No. 63 bus goes past the door. It is accessible for the disabled.
The various papers for the meeting are attached.
If any member would like a lift, or to arrange for a babysitter on our rota system, please contact me; my phone number is xxx xxxx.
Looking forward to seeing you there.
Best wishes,
Tony Odie

The agenda

Agenda is a Latin word which means 'to be done'. So the agenda is the list of items which have got to be discussed at a meeting. Some organizations only give a series of headings on one sheet of paper and perhaps refer you to other documents. For instance, an agenda could say: 'Item 3. Purchase of new van (see attached report)'.

Other agendas include the issues to be covered in the agenda itself, so the same item could read instead: 'Item 3. Purchase of new van. The secretary has investigated this and obtained the following quotes . . . The committee are asked to decide between the alternatives.'

Motions (see p. 107) can be on the main agenda or on a separate sheet. The advantage of the first, short style, is that it makes it easier to follow where the meeting is at any time; the disadvantage is that you have to shuffle a lot of paper around. If you get the papers in the wrong order, you could be completely lost, so it is important that they are numbered clearly at the top. Tony likes the short style; so his agenda reads:

AGENDA
1. Apologies for absence.
2. Minutes of the last meeting (attached).
3. Matters arising from the minutes (see paper 1 attached).
4. Correspondence.
5. Reports:
   (a) Executive Committee;
   (b) from councillors;
   (c) from delegate to Annual Conference.
6. Talk by Anne Brown.
7. Motions (see attached paper 2).
8. Date of next meeting.
9. Any other business.

As you will see, Tony has told people what papers are attached to the agenda, which makes it easy to check if you've got everything.

A less formal group might put only the main points down, perhaps incorporating them in the letter which tells you the arrangements for the meeting, as described on p. 85. So the middle paragraph of that letter could read, 'We will be discussing, among other things, the reports from our councillors and our delegate to Annual Conference, and Anne Brown, from the National Executive, is going to speak.' Then you could finalize the agenda at the beginning of the meeting itself (see p. 100). If you do it this way, try to get the papers that are going to be discussed out in good time – people will still need to read them in advance.

Some groups will send out just the formal notice and a brief agenda like this in good time for the meeting, and either send all the documents that are to be considered later, or give them to you when you get there. This means that you know when and where the meeting is, but it still does not give you proper time to read the documents. Having two separate mailings adds to the chances of people leaving some of the papers at home. Sometimes, however, the secretary can't help sending out some of the papers late, as s/he is let down by someone else who does not turn up with material at the right time.

Minutes of last meeting

Minutes are the notes of what happened at the last meeting. These are discussed in more detail on pp. 111–17. Usually the minutes of the last meeting are sent out with the notice of the next one, but they may go out before that if there is a long gap. Some groups hand out the minutes at the time of the next meeting, but this means people do not have time to read them properly, so try to avoid this.

In other groups the secretary reads them out laboriously to the meeting. This used to be a common practice. Presumably it developed in the days before photocopiers and duplicators, when it would have been very difficult for a working-class organization to make enough copies for everyone. Since this is no longer the case, people ought to be given their own copy to read, if it is within your group's resources.

If you are unable to send a copy to every member, you might be able to arrange for a local representative to pin one up on the noticeboard in the workplace or other meeting place, and also have sufficient copies available at the meeting for everyone who is there to collect one at the beginning.

Reports

As you can see from the example of an agenda, there are several different sorts of reports to come up, and the papers to be sent out may well look different. The report from a committee could be simply the minutes of that committee, which the meeting would then go through, while the report from a councillor, or the delegate to a conference, could be a page or so of description of what happened.

Often, reports are not put in writing, but the person concerned simply talks about the subject. Writing down the report in advance, however,

- makes him/her consider the issue more thoroughly;
- gives the members a chance to think about the issues and what questions they want to ask;
- ought to avoid the need at the meeting to spend a lot of time listening to a report about which no one's very interested. If you have a written report the chair can simply ask, 'Has anyone got a question?' and, if not, move on to the next item.

Prising reports out of people in time to send them out is not easy. In fact it can be the worst part of the secretary's job. Sometimes you may have to hand reports out at the meeting itself. This means that the secretary, or someone else, has to remember to bring enough copies with him/her for the people who turn up. Try to avoid this if possible.

Preparations

If possible, the chair and secretary should talk about the meeting, at least on the phone, a day or two beforehand. They should check:

- who is covering what points;
- how long each item is likely to take;
- any likely arguments or procedural difficulties, and ways of handling them.

There is a thin line, not always easy to draw, between this sort of pre-discussion and manipulation of the meeting. The chair and secretary **ought** to be thinking about the issues that are going to be raised and how they should be coped with in terms of the time allowed and the rules to be followed. If it becomes more than that – if they start planning ways of stifling the discussion or carving up jobs – the members should recognize the dangers of this and discourage them strongly.

Having thought about the issues that are coming up, either the chair or secretary should make time to draft a 'timed' agenda. That is, beside each item on the agenda s/he puts the time the meeting ought to get to that item if it's going to cover everything. This can only be provisional, and if you stick to it too rigidly you risk upsetting people, but it does give some guidance on how long you can let people go on without creating problems later about dealing with equally important questions.

So Cheryl, the chair of Tony's branch, writes down on her agenda:

AGENDA – aim to start by 8.05

1. Apologies for absence; 8.05.
2. Minutes of the last meeting; 8.07.
3. Matters arising from the minutes; 8.10.
4. Correspondence; 8.30.
5. Reports; 8.40.
6. Talk by Anne Brown; 9.10.
7. Resolutions; 9.40.
8. Election of delegate to area council; 9.45.
9. Date of next meeting; 9.50.
10. Any other business; 9.55.

Close meeting at 10 p.m.

In some groups, the timings are included in the agenda that is sent out to the members. Theoretically this should make them appreciate more the need to keep the discussion limited so that they have time to consider everything; but in practice it doesn't happen and people still go on at enormous length. Another possibility is to announce at the beginning of the meeting the timings you are suggesting and ask people to stick to them.

Before the meeting, the secretary must get together all the papers, and the people, that are going to be needed. So Tony would make sure he had

- got copies of the minutes of the last meeting;
- either asked people to talk about the lobby of the council and the fund-raising social, or checked on the position himself so he can talk;
- got together all the letters, both to the branch and from it, that need reporting under 'correspondence';
- sorting out who is giving what report, and confirmed that they are coming;
- checked that Anne Brown is coming, and knows how to get there;
- thought about a date for the next meeting, if it's not a fixed one.

Even if all the papers have been sent out in advance, there will always be people who've forgotten to bring theirs, so it's sensible to bring a few spare copies of each one with you for those people to pick up.

Tony would also need to check that the hall had been booked, and any refreshments, bookstall, or other items that were being provided had been organized, with people to look after them. In other words, the secretary is usually the dogsbody who does the work of getting things ready. There is no reason, though, why the one person should have to do everything. The chair could take on some tasks, or other people in the group could be asked to do specific things, but it is the secretary's job to co-ordinate everything.

One or two individuals, perhaps the chair and secretary, or perhaps another person given this particular job, must be at the meeting place **early**, to make sure that it is open and welcoming. Punctuality is something people are quite bad at, and those involved in 'non-formal' meetings can be worse than those in formal ones. If people turn up and find things unprepared, perhaps even the hall locked and no one around, they are quite likely to leave, afraid they have come on the wrong night or to the wrong place. Any group will run better if someone has taken the trouble to get things ready in advance.

Participation

Chapter 5 looks at ways of running meetings without the formal procedures. Although this chapter covers meetings that do have such procedures, there are, even so, ways of making it easier for people to take part; this section looks at some of them.

Preparations

For most formal meetings, the chairs are arranged in rows across the hall and there is a table with two or three chairs behind it at the front for the officers. This is very intimidating; it looks as if you have strayed into a church. If there is no other change you can make, you could try at least to get the room to look more friendly. Try

- putting the chairs in a circle, one row or several rows deep, depending on how big your meeting is;
- for a meeting where you're going to break into smaller groups (see p. 92), arranging sets of chairs round smaller tables;
- for a larger meeting, placing chairs in an irregular fan shape.

The person making notes will find it much easier if s/he has a table to rest on. The person chairing the meeting may find it easier too, but s/he does not actually need a table and removing it is a good way to break down the barriers between the chair and the other officers, so try, if possible, to do without it.

Think also, preferably in advance so you can do something about it, about what sort of image people will get of your organization.

- How does the room feel? You may not have much choice, as not every hall will allow you to put things up on the wall, but, if you can, try to brighten the place up and make it relate more to your group, perhaps by pinning up your latest posters, having a stall with booklets, badges, T-shirts and anything else your group has to sell.
- Can you offer tea and coffee at the beginning? You could also provide it during a break, if it's a long meeting. Providing alcohol is not a very good idea, unless there is little business and it is more of a social occasion, since it tends to make people talkative and argumentative. Keep the wine until the end.

Before the meeting has actually started, while people are coming in, what happens when a new person appears? Is everyone in a little huddle at one end of the room, and turns round to stare? Do they simply ignore new people, who may start wondering if they are invisible? Instead, try to be welcoming. Someone should go over to the new person to say hello, introduce himself/herself and explain what is happening, and generally help make him/her feel at home. This needs to be a deliberately established policy to work, as otherwise the regulars can feel as embarrassed as the new person. If you are rotating tasks, as suggested in Chapter 3, it could be another job to be given to one specific person at each meeting.

Introductions

At any meeting where there are new faces, people should go round and announce their names at the beginning. It can also be useful for them to make name cards, by writing the name they like to be called in large letters on a piece of paper, and folding it so that it stands up and people can read it.

If your group is meeting for the first time, or if there is a substantial group of new people, even though some of you may know each other quite well, spend a little more time on this. It will help to break the ice, as well as enable people to get to know each other more quickly.

One possible method is for each person to say a few words about themselves, who they are, why they've come, what they want to get out of the meeting, at the beginning to everyone else. This can be fairly nerve-racking for a shy person, and therefore disliked by many people.

As an alternative, try 'paired introductions'. This means that each person interviews the one next to him/her asking for his/her details. The other one does the same and then each one tells the rest of the group about the person s/he's interviewed. This has the advantage that it means you get chatting with one person early on, so that face is familiar even if the others remain strange. It takes time, however. Allow about 10 minutes for the initial pairing, plus two or three minutes each for the reporting back. This needs to be fitted in with everything else you have to cover.

If you don't have time for either of these, at least the people chairing the meeting and taking notes should introduce themselves at the beginning, and anyone else who speaks should also say who s/he is.

Discussions

Most of the discussions at labour movement meetings are very uninspiring, and those taking part learn very little, because they are set pieces. People come with their prepared speeches, make them without taking account of what has already been said and without the chance to discuss them after something else has been said, and so go away with their opinions unchanged. Others feel too timid to say anything at all, especially if they are not quite sure of where they stand, because the speech-makers are so very definite and there seems very little room for a 'perhaps'. For others, the idea of standing up and making your voice carry in a big meeting is too daunting. How can you make it easier for people to join in?

- The way the seats are arranged can make a surprising difference. If they are in rows, so people have their backs to you, if you talk from where you are sitting, then you've got to be loud to be heard. Alternatively, you may have to go up to the front and stand there, like a teacher before a class. If the chairs are in a circle or a fan shape, many more people can see or hear you and you do not need to be so loud and therefore so aggressive-sounding.
- You don't need to have all thc discussion in one big meeting. As was pointed out on p. 62, remaining as a single group, once the numbers go beyond five or six, is quite difficult and can be a strain. There may be points during the meeting where you could break into smaller groups, perhaps of four or five. These can then discuss the issue informally, without people feeling as shy as they do in a large group; therefore they may be more willing to talk. Those whose habit is to make long eloquent speeches to a mass audience may also feel that these are out of place, and hopefully not talk so much.

Dividing into groups is a method that is often used in adult education. It can be very successful, but it does take a lot of time and it can lead to discussions which are just as boring and profitless as any other, if not properly prepared. To work well, each group needs a carefully defined 'task' and to be told what the aim behind it is. Therefore, someone must take on the job of preparing the material for this. People will need:

- background information;
- a list of points to answer, written clearly and in a way that is not going to confuse anyone about what exactly is meant.

■ One local Labour Party decided to use this as a means of working out what to say when canvassing during the European elections. So one person wrote out 'activity sheets' for each group, which said:

Here is a list of points that might come up on the doorstep when you are canvassing. As a group, work out how to respond, put your answers on a flipchart and appoint someone to report back to the whole meeting.

Points:

1. But Labour's against the Market, isn't it?

2. I'm not going to bother – it won't make any difference.
3. I don't hold with the Common Market – we should never have gone in, so I'm not going to vote.

The meeting divided into groups of five or six, and discussed the questions for about half an hour; they put a list of the replies they had thought of on 'flipcharts' – poster-sized pieces of paper which they then stuck on the walls. Then the whole meeting got back together again, and one person from each group explained the flipcharts to everyone else, and they had a general discussion, based on these, for another half hour. Afterwards, someone typed up a list of the points that had been made, both on the flipcharts and in the discussion, and gave copies to everyone who'd taken part, for use during the elections.

One reason that people use this method in adult education is that you learn better by doing something than by listening to someone else explaining how to do it. You have to concentrate more, and so you will remember more afterwards. So a small group session is particularly good for going over arguments you'll need to use later. It's also useful for coming up with ideas if the group as a whole seems to have run out of ideas or if people are feeling at a dead end.

There are other methods too, such as 'brainstorming'. This means that for five minutes you sit in a group and each person throws out all the ideas that come into his/her head on, say, fund-raising. One person stands in front of a blackboard or flipchart and writes them all down. At the end of the time, you have a long list, some of the ideas silly, some sensible, and you go through crossing out the silly ones, and use the sensible ones as the basis for a longer discussion. It gets people's brains working and can help you to see things in a less limited way.

The initial thinking about resolutions can also be done in small groups. You may have to send something in for your conference; various people may have some vague ideas, but no one has a clear proposal. Those with ideas could be asked to name the subject they are thinking about, and those who are interested could join their group and hammer out a resolution in detailed discussion. You still have the problem of deciding between the different groups' proposals, but far more people should have had the chance of looking at one issue, at least, than if you have a series of short debates with prepared speeches.

Speakers

The conventional ways of coping with an invited speaker at a meeting are discussed on pp. 105–6. There are other ways of doing this, but before your group tries any of them they may need convincing of the need.

These are some problems about having an outside speaker.

- People may feel intimidated by having an 'expert' there and not willing to show their ignorance of the subject in front of them, so they simply keep quiet.
- The speaker may be biased on one side or the other, and unable to appreciate that some people are uncertain or undecided. If anyone expresses doubts, s/he may treat those people with scorn and be unwilling to listen to the arguments on the other side, even when people are putting them in order to work things out for themselves.
- There are speakers – only too many – who do not actually know all that much. They are skilled in presentation, and in public speaking, rather than in the facts, so it is difficult to learn anything in depth from them.

The advantage of having a speaker, especially a well-known one, is that s/he may draw new people to your meeting. An alternative is to ask one or two of your own members to go away and find out about a subject. Or you could invite an outsider, but change the **order** of the meetings round.

As explained on pp. 105–6, it is usually taken for granted that first the speaker talks, then you ask questions and s/he replies, then s/he summarizes the discussion, someone 'moves a vote of thanks' (see p. 106) and the speaker goes away. This means that the speaker comes in cold, not knowing how much information you already have or what your attitudes are. S/he may pitch things entirely wrong, therefore, assuming either that you know more than you do and so going over your heads, or thinking that you know very little and so wasting your time telling you what you already know.

Instead you could have a discussion **before** the speaker starts, perhaps in smaller groups, and decide on what questions you want to ask. Then tell the speaker, asking him/her to make sure these points are covered in the talk; then the questions afterwards can concentrate on getting obscure matters clear, or pursuing a particular issue further.

It's best to warn a speaker in advance if you intend to do this, because some people would find it very difficult to move away from a prepared speech, especially if they are nervous themselves. Ask if they can provide you with a note of the main factual points, perhaps just one side of a page, so that people can read it before they start discussing in small groups. So for a discussion on Ireland, for example, you could have a note of:

- the population, and the proportions of Catholics and Protestants;
- the unemployment level;
- the dates of important events like Partition, and internment;
- an explanation of your organization's previous policy decisions.

People could get together, again in groups of four or five, for about 10 minutes before the speaker begins, and the first five minutes of his/her time would be taken up listening to members' comments.

Another possibility for informing yourselves about a subject is to have an 'audio-visual' – a film, a video or a tape/slide show – first, and then a discussion after it. Many good videos come with discussion notes for people to use, or one person could be asked to prepare some ideas. It will be easier if one person is asked to lead the discussion, especially at the beginning, when people are still blinking as the lights go up, as they can be fairly slow to get off the ground.

For details of how to get hold of films and videos, and the equipment needed to go with it, see *Organising Things* p. 201–7 (details in Further Reading, p. 210). Be warned, however: a bad audio-visual is worse than useless. It leaves people feeling tired, with eyestrain or confused and irritated.

An increasing number of good videos made for the labour movement are now available – a number were made for the 1984–5 miners' strike, for example – so you should not be satisfied with anything that is less than good.

Taking part

At some point people who are just getting involved in a group are going to have to open their mouths for the first time. The larger the group, and the more formal the proceedings, the more frightening this is. It is not possible to give a complete guide to speaking here, but a few points may help.

- Get prepared in advance. Do some research, check your facts, and write out a series of headings on a piece of paper or several postcards.
- Keep what you're saying brief and relevant.
- When you start talking, speak to the people furthest away. Make eye contact with the people at the back of the room if

you're standing at the front, and talk as if they're the only people in the room. Your voice will be heard by everyone else. If you're looking at individuals, you'll be able to see if they don't understand or are bored.

- Remember that the first time is always the worst.

At the end of the meeting

When the meeting ends, some people will immediately rush off to the pub. Others will hang around talking, selling their newspapers, asking people to sign petitions, and so on.

Someone has a certain amount of dogsbody work to do clearing up after the meeting; this is usually the secretary, who should try to get some help, not slog on alone.

At this stage, as much as at the beginning, it is important to think about how friendly the group is to new or unconfident people. If you all go off to the pub or a café, people need **to go with** the new members, not expect them to find their own way. Someone should ask

- how they felt;
- whether there were points they didn't understand;
- whether language was used that was unclear.

It's very easy for the 'old hands' to get into huddles in the corner and re-fight battles, go over the points that have already been discussed, or just start gossiping about friends and acquaintances. The more the group functions at a social level as well as a business one, the easier it is to fall into this trap. You need to be conscious enough about this to include the new person in your conversation quite deliberately to start with, although after a while it should become easy and natural.

It is also useful for someone – perhaps the person who has taken the chair this time – to do a lot of listening afterwards, especially where the meeting is a large one. That is, s/he should go round the various groups listening to what they have to say and how they feel. If a lot is being said that ought to have come out at the meeting, and people are saying, 'I didn't like to say this in front of the others but . . .', that is a danger signal. Were they frightened to say things publicly? Who were they afraid of, and why? If there are people showing hostility to each other, perhaps resenting something that was said earlier, that can create problems; why did they not say something? A non-formal structure, especially, ought to allow for these feelings to be expressed and then got out of the way. If they are allowed to fester, they can be more dangerous to the structure than in the formal set-up.

The roles of chair and secretary

It's already been suggested (see p. 64) that the tasks of the chair and secretary should rotate among different members, and this point is covered again on p. 118. However, this section looks only at the roles in a formally run meeting.

The essential points, for the person in the chair, are:

- to know what is being discussed, and keep people from wandering off on to other, irrelevant points;
- to end the discussion and move on to the next subject, when agreement is reached, or everyone knows where the disagreement is;
- to make sure that people who want to speak are given the chance and that people do not cut across and interrupt.

The last point is probably the most difficult. People put up their hands, or catch the chair's eye, to show that they wish to speak, and it's then the chair's job to tell them to go ahead. Usually this is in the order in which they showed that they wanted to talk, although if someone wished to react to something that was being said about him/her, or had to leave early, that person could be allowed to jump the queue. Some people, however, will not wait their turn, but leap into any gap, so the chair has to ask them to hold back. Others may interrupt while someone is actually talking, and the chair must then tell them to stop.

This may sound a bit daunting, and it can be, at a bad-tempered meeting, if there are people who are determined to dominate. However, if you are seen to be fair, the rest of the meeting will almost certainly support you against a challenge.

The other side of this is that if the chair is not fair, s/he will irritate the rest. If you let your friends speak and ignore others, or if you dominate the meeting yourself and say something after each person speaks, you will tend to lose sympathy and find people becoming awkward.

At the end of a discussion on any item, the chair should try to spell out briefly what has been decided, make sure the meeting agrees on it and move on to the next point. Doing this makes it easy for the secretary to keep accurate notes (see pp. 111–17).

Taking and recording decisions

These are some of the most important functions of the officers. When the chair or secretary knows there is a decision to be taken, s/he must point this out to everyone else. If there is an item on which people begin to have a discussion, the chair must ensure that they don't simply ramble on, but come to a definite view about what should be done.

Under 'matters arising', for instance, there could be four points listed on the agenda, and there might be others that the secretary does not know anyone intends to mention. But these two points might simply be reports on what's happening, or people might need to take a decision.

For example, Harry Smith might tell you when the lobby of the council has been arranged, ask you all to do your best to get there, and all the members will nod and agree. The secretary would put in the minutes that this was **noted**. Harry might then say that he thought the branch banner should be taken along. In a formally run meeting, this would have to be **proposed** and **seconded** (see pp. 39–40). You might have a discussion about it or agree to it straight away.

The next point is often forgotten in these highly formal, custom-bound meetings: deciding **who** is going to take the banner along. Except for things that are trivial or quite obvious, the chair ought not to start on the next item until it's clear how the last decision is going to be carried out. In this case, Cheryl should ask for volunteers, and perhaps tell them to meet the secretary afterwards to collect the banner. The secretary meanwhile would write in the notes, 'It was proposed by . . . and seconded by . . . and carried by xx votes to xx to take the branch banner on the lobby. Fred and Mary agreed to be responsible for it and the secretary arranged to hand it over afterwards.'

This means that the members know, even if they are not at the meeting, what the task was and who is responsible if something goes wrong. Perhaps at the next meeting, under 'matters arising', someone will ask, 'Were Fred and Mary there? I never saw the banner.' Fred would then have to explain that his car broke down and they never got there.

Having a decision properly recorded also safeguards the individuals involved. If Fred and Mary took the branch's valuable banner and it then got smashed up by the police, the branch might feel they had not taken proper care of it, but they could be in no doubt that they were authorized to take it, because the minutes say they were.

The meeting itself

Credentials

At many meetings, for instance of trade-union branches, people have to show either their membership card or their **credentials** at the door. A credential can be a card you show at each meeting, or a slip of paper. This may be on the bottom of the agenda so that you tear it off, or it could be separate, in which case it tends to fall out of the envelope and get lost, so that you need to check that you have it before setting out to the meeting.

Having credentials can be important if the group is going to take policy decisions on behalf of a lot of other people. They ensure that the people there all have authority to take decisions and that the meeting isn't being taken over secretly by people who are not representative and can't speak for anyone. If a Labour Party is selecting a new candidate to stand as MP, for instance, it matters considerably that everyone who gets in to the meeting is entitled to be there. Where there could be legal problems later, this may be crucial. (See Chapter 10 for more on this.)

In other instances, credentials are not necessary; you might be asked to sign a book or a sheet of paper during the meeting to show you were there. Sometimes the book doesn't get round the whole room and the people at the back may need to ask for it.

The person who stands or sits at the door, checking the credentials as people come in, is often called the **doorkeeper**. S/he should have a list of all those who are entitled to attend, so that anyone who has forgotten to bring the right papers but can prove who they are can still get in. At a big meeting the doorkeeper will be helped by **stewards**, who are there to tell people where their seats and the other facilities are, and generally keep order.

Calling the meeting to order

The meeting will usually not be able to start until there is a **quorum**, that is, at least a certain number of members there. This, and what happens when you don't have a quorum, is explained on pp. 22–3.

When there are enough people, the chair needs to 'call the meeting to order'. According to Citrine, the chair should have a little wooden hammer, called a 'gavel', to bang on its stand and get people's attention. Many organizations have these gavels, which are often quite old and beautifully made. Alternatively, s/he may shout or bang something on the table.

The chair will often start off by saying, 'Order, order. I declare this meeting open.' This is jargon lifted straight from parliamentary procedure. Another way of saying it is, 'Will the comrades/delegates/members please **come to order**?' Either way, the meaning is, 'Please stop your private conversations and listen to what I'm saying.'

The agenda

If there is already an agenda which has been circulated in advance (see p. 86), the chair begins by simply going through it. If anyone wants to change the order in which items are to be taken, this is the time for them to say so. If you want to add an item, or make sure something is coming up, this is the right time to do it. In some groups, the chair asks what items are to be covered in 'any other business' (see p. 110) at this point, so that if anyone wants to raise something, they must remember to mention it.

If you are drawing up your agenda at the meeting itself, then this is your first task. Try to put things down, either on a notepad or on a blackboard or a large piece of paper on the wall; aim to put them in an order which means that you don't leap around from subject to subject. Try to decide how long each item is going to take, so that you know whether you are going to get through everything.

Apologies for absence

The first formal item on the agenda is usually apologies for absence. The secretary reads out a list of all those who have said that they are unable to come. Anyone who's heard about someone else not coming will also add their names, and the secretary writes these down in the **minutes**.

It can be important to send in your apologies if you can't go to a meeting, and to make sure that they are put down. As explained on p. 17, in many groups, if you miss more than a certain number of meetings without sending in apologies, you can lose your place.

Minutes

Next will come the minutes of the last meeting. There are two ways of dealing with these. Either the chair can assume that everyone has read them and immediately ask, 'Are these a correct record?' Or the secretary can read them out, while everyone else listens. This second method puts a great strain on the memory and great power in the hands of the secretary, so it is better, if possible, to have copies sent out in advance, or at least circulated at the meeting (see p. 86).

Even if the minutes have been circulated, in some groups it is the habit that the secretary starts to read them out and then someone interrupts and says, 'Move that the minutes be taken as read.' This means, 'Let's assume that the secretary has read out the minutes already.'

If at every meeting there is this formality, the chair or a member could suggest that the procedure is changed for good. This could involve changing the **standing orders**, in which case you would have to check how this was done (see Chapter 2). It could, however, be merely a custom that has grown up, which would be simpler to alter.

The next formal step is for the chair to ask whether the minutes are a **correct record**. This means that everyone agrees the minutes are accurate. Once this has been done, you cannot then object that you never said what they record you as saying, or that you weren't at the meeting anyway.

To make the minutes official in the eyes of the law, they must be signed and dated by the chair; any alterations made because the minute-taker got it wrong must be initialled. For most organizations, the law does not really matter, but even so it is good practice to make sure there is one copy of the minutes, perhaps kept in a special book, so that everyone knows what is the correct version. The auditors (see p. 28) may wish to see them anyway, when they are checking the accounts.

If a member thinks that the minutes are wrong, s/he would say at this point, for example, 'I propose that item 4(a) be amended. The treasurer reported that we had £50 in the bank, not £500.' The chair would probably then ask if that proposal was seconded (see p. 40). This would mean that someone else agreed that the minutes were wrong. There could be a short discussion about it – although this should be kept as brief as possible, so that you can move quickly on to new questions. There might have to be a vote.

If other people agreed that was correct, the chair would then ask if that amendment was accepted, and make the change if it was.

If a controversial issue is being dealt with, exactly what the minutes say can be important and can mean a long-drawn-out wrangle. More often, there has been a simple misunderstanding or a typing error, and it can be quickly put right, so there is no need for a vote.

The point to bear in mind here is the order in which you do things. First, you decide if the minutes are an accurate report of what went on. Only after that do you discuss the subject itself, under matters arising.

Matters arising

This covers points that were discussed at the last meeting, when perhaps someone was asked to do some work, or there's been a subsequent development. So, for instance, the secretary of your Labour Party branch might have been asked to write to the local MP about something; s/he might report that this had been done, but that there hadn't yet been a reply.

If there had been one, though, it might be covered under correspondence (see p. 102), or be an item all on its own. In this case, when the meeting is going through the minutes, the secretary should say, 'Under item 3, the reply from Jo Bloggs MP will be coming up later.' If s/he doesn't, it's sensible to ask when this item will be coming up, just to be certain that it will be covered somewhere. So someone might say, if the secretary doesn't mention it, 'Under item 3, is there a reply from Jo Bloggs MP?' The secretary can then say, 'Yes, and the matter will be coming up under correspondence.'

If there are several items which the secretary knows have to be reported to the meeting, there might be a list under matters arising. Alternatively, they may be separate items. This depends on the style the organization has developed. Some meetings spend half their time on 'matters arising', and it can be here that all the real discussion takes place. With a weak chair, it can also give an opportunity for endlessly re-opening discussion on things people thought were settled last time, and also allow for considerable obstruction if people raise a lot of points about the minutes in order to avoid getting on to the real business. The best thing is for the secretary to pick out the items over which there is obviously going to be further discussion and put them on the agenda as a separate item, or as a subheading, and a good chair should then stop the meeting discussing them until the right point.

In the example of Tony Odie's agenda on p. 86, he could have written down:

Matters arising:
(a) lobby of council
(b) Xmas bazaar
(c) letter to MP
(d) any other.

If you are told something is coming up later, keep your eyes open to make sure it does. There is a scene in a Groucho Marx film where people try to raise an item and are first told it's too soon, that it is coming up later; when they raise it later they're told it's too late, that the item's passed. This is not unknown in real life!

If the minutes are long and complicated, once it's been agreed they are correct, they may be taken **paragraph by paragraph**, or **page by page**. The chair reads out the heading of each paragraph, or just the number, and you have to make your point before s/he continues. If you are diffident about shouting out or raising your hand, you can lose the opportunity. You may be able to apologize and ask the chair to return to that item, but this will irritate others. It helps to go through the minutes and the other documents first, and mark the places where you want to say something.

Correspondence

This is usually the next item on the agenda, although sometimes it comes much later. It means all the letters that have been received by the organization since the last meeting. They can be dealt with in different ways. If your group does not receive many letters, the secretary may read them all out to the meeting before they are discussed. If, on the other hand, there are a lot, sometimes they are listed in a separate 'correspondence list' sent out with the agenda, or given to people who come to the meetings. One Labour Party branch, for instance, has a list like this:

Correspondence: Executive Committee meeting 17.1.84

Letter	**Suggested Action**
Party leader rally 7.2.84	Circulate
GLC panel of candidates	Circulate
Labour Party merit awards	None
Labour Party B list	Ask branches
Co-op election sponsorship	Note
GLC transport meeting 11.2.84	General Committee to appoint delegate
Affiliation fees	Decision needed
Bill Brown, resignation from EC	Write thanking

The secretary has put down all the letters received and suggested what should happen to them. The chair then goes through this list, and asks the secretary, or someone else, to explain the headings more fully and then says, 'Does the committee agree we should circulate this letter to branches?' or whatever the proposal may be.

If it's an important or controversial issue, you may want to have a detailed discussion and someone might propose something else, for example, that the letter be 'noted' (see p. 53). This would need proposing and seconding, and you could end up voting on it in the same way as you do for a resolution.

Another method of dealing with letters is to put them in a folder and pass this round the meeting so that everyone can read them. However, this means that the people sitting at the back won't see the folder until late, perhaps after correspondence has been dealt with on the agenda. It might be possible to say something about a letter under any other business (see p. 110) but it would mean going back over old ground. It's better, if this method is used, to put correspondence to be dealt with later in the agenda.

Any really important letters, perhaps one including the details of a wage offer or a controversial statement someone's made, should, if possible, be circulated in advance, or at least enough copies should be made to hand out to people at the meeting.

Frequently a combination of methods is used, with items treated in different ways depending on their importance. For example:

- head office circulars might be listed, and copies made available for anyone who wants to take them away;
- replies to letters written on behalf of the organization, or other letters the secretary wants to draw attention to, might be read out.

Items may not be reported, or they may be put in the wrong place, so you need to keep your eyes open. It is not necessarily a deliberate mistake; the secretary may not realize the relevance of a particular item. Perhaps a letter from your MP is being circulated in the file; but you may feel that it raises an important issue and should be more fully discussed. If you know in advance that an important letter is to be sent to the secretary, you could write or phone him/her in advance and make sure that it is going to be reported properly to the meeting. If you think that something is being deliberately overlooked, doing this would give the secretary no excuse for omitting it.

As the letters are gone through, the secretary must make a note of what's to be done with each one. Some people write on the letter itself, or on the back of it. Another possibility is that if you have a list like the one described on p. 103, you can put notes beside that, or you could write a list as you go along, perhaps numbering each letter. It's important to identify clearly each letter as you go along, as otherwise it may not be obvious, when you read back your notes later, whether you are supposed to reply to the head office letter or another in a particular way.

There is no formally laid-down procedure for this; it is a matter of evolving by trial and error the most efficient way to operate, given that the most important business coming up at a meeting is often included in a letter.

One way to liven up a meeting is to divide up the letters that need reading out or summarizing among various people in the group and ask them to carry out this task when you reach it. This has the advantages of:

- changing voices – it is very dull to listen to the same person's voice all the time;
- giving different people a definite job to do;
- giving the secretary a rest from the dual role of reading and writing.

At the least, another committee member could do the reading, if not an ordinary member of the group.

Reports

How reports are dealt with is covered on pp. 52–4. The problem for the chair is stopping people giving reports from going on too long. If the report has already been written down, there should be no need to go over the same ground again, although you may not be able to prevent it. Each person giving a report should be asked to supply the main points and add anything important. Try to prevent them from repeating everything that's already been written down. After perhaps a five-minute introduction, people should be asked if they want to ask questions or raise issues. The jargon phrase is that the report is 'thrown open to the meeting'.

If it is a report on which you are being asked to make decisions, for instance, the proposals of a subcommittee, the chair should go 'paragraph by paragraph', as with the minutes (see p. 102), to give you a chance to say something on each item. In some reports of this sort, a star may be put beside the items where a decision has to be made. The chair should clearly understand the powers of the group reporting back (checking if necessary with the constitution) and should not let the people to whom they are reporting tread on their toes. For instance, if the schools subcommittee has the job of appointing school governors, and some of the general committee don't like the governors they've appointed, the chair should not let them propose to change the decision the subcommittee has already made. S/he should rule that **out of order** (see p. 55). If they wanted to show they were annoyed, they could propose a **vote of censure** for that decision. This is in order because it's telling them off for it, but not trying to change it.

This may seem like a bureaucratic quibble, but there is a point to it. A group will not work well if it doesn't know what its job is, or if whenever it gets on with something, it finds that it is constantly interfered with and questions that have already been dealt with are taken up again so that nothing is ever finished. If one committee is allowed to tread on another's toes, there is a risk that the people who like to dominate will be able to take over more and more, including areas in which they are not supposed to be involved, and no one will be able to stop them because they have acted in the same way in the past themselves.

Visiting speakers

Many groups decide to have a speaker at their meetings as a matter of course, without thinking too much about it. Largely as a result of this, what could be a very useful exercise – picking the brains of an expert – often becomes rather boring.

If someone is coming in to talk, then in the conventional meeting what **ought** to happen is that s/he is asked to come at a particular time, told how long the group would like him/her to speak and how long to answer questions, and then the meeting sticks to that.

Unfortunately, this frequently does not happen. Anne Brown may be asked to come at 8.30 p.m. and does so, only to find the meeting still wrangling over the minutes of the last meeting. She sits in the corner feeling annoyed, and finally the wrangle breaks off long enough to allow Anne to say her piece and answer questions. Sometimes the speaker finds himself/herself squeezed right to the end of the business, with much less time than s/he has been led to expect. Half the audience may be shuffling their feet and looking at watches; they may even leave during the speech. Labour movement groups can often be very rude and offhand to people who might have gone to quite a lot of trouble. It's not intentional, it's just that people don't think.

On the other hand, speakers can be equally difficult and rude. They often don't turn up on time and, having started speaking, they go on much longer than you've asked them to, so that they either leave very little time for questions or mess up the rest of your business.

Before a group decides to have a speaker, think about how much other business there is to get through. If there is too much, then either postpone some of it, or don't invite anyone (alternatively you could work out why everything is taking so long). Once you have decided to invite someone, then the chair should:

- break off the other discussion at the time you've said you will;
- make sure the speaker knows how much time is available. About five minutes before it is going to run out, the chair should pass over a note saying, in large letters, 'Five minutes more, please', and then, a minute before, 'One minute more, please', and finally, one saying, 'Will you wind up now?' if the speaker is still carrying on.

It is, however, almost impossible to stop a guest speaker who insists on going over time, without being really rude. It would involve actually cutting off the person in full flight, perhaps even turning off the microphone if you have one. It is best not to try unless it really is necessary; you just have to resign yourself.

After the person has spoken, you then have perhaps half an hour's questions and discussion on the subject. Often the chair will ask for people to ask factual questions first, before you start discussing the issue. This is logical, but it doesn't work in practice as people immediately start giving their opinions. Ordinary members may also go on at great length, unless the chair restrains them, thus leaving very little time either for the speaker to reply or for other people to come in.

The chair's job, during the questions and discussion, is to look out for people who want to say something and try to give them a chance, in the order in which they put up their hands. In a big hall, it can be quite hard to see everyone, so it helps to have someone else on the platform as well, pointing people out. Women tend to be overlooked, even by women chairs, so a conscious effort should be made to be fair. Usually people are not allowed a second chance until everyone who wants to speak once has had a chance to do so. This is fair, but it does tend to prevent a coherent discussion developing. If there's a particularly important issue being raised, or if the speaker is obviously evading a question, the chair can always use his/her judgement to let the same person come in again.

A good chair takes very little part in the discussion himself/herself, leaving it to everyone else. This can be frustrating if there are things the chair wants to say, but unless s/he holds back it will irritate other people and they will feel, whether it's true or not, that the chair is abusing his/her position to express a particular point of view.

There are some speakers – and some chairs – who speak at length after every contribution, but this is not a good practice.

Votes of thanks

At the end of the time arranged for a discussion, it's polite to thank the speaker. This can be done by the chair, but often it is done by a formal procedure; the chair 'calls for a vote of thanks'. Usually someone has been tipped off at the beginning to do this. It involves standing up and making a short speech saying how delighted you are that Anne Brown could be with you tonight, how much you enjoyed the speech, and so on. It does not matter if it isn't true, no one believes it anyway. People sometimes use it as an opportunity to make sly digs at other people. The proposer ends the speech with, 'I therefore move a vote of thanks', and the chair then says, 'Is that agreed?' and everyone says yes, or claps. There are not usually other speakers or a proper vote on this; it would be too embarrassing if the vote were turned down.

It is an unnecessary formal procedure, but it is not really worth making a fuss about it.

Motions

The way in which these are dealt with is covered on pp. 37–42. If there are a lot of motions, one way of speeding up the business is to see if any of them are 'non-contentious', that is, the sort that no one disagrees with. These can be passed 'on the nod', that is, without a debate, or with only the proposer explaining the resolution.

The chair can ask, when the item comes up, 'Is the motion opposed?' If it is not, there is no need for a vote. The chair can simply ask if it is agreed. Many groups insist on voting on everything, however, and in that case, the chair can then ask, 'Shall I put it to the vote?' and do so provided that no one disagrees. However, be cautious about this, as people might not have had a chance to take in the full implications of something, or they might want to discuss the issue anyway.

Once a motion is passed, it becomes a **resolution**. What happens to the resolutions after they're passed? If they just sit in the files, there's not a lot of point in passing them. Unless it's clear from the resolution itself, the chair needs to ask each time, 'Where should this be sent?' At a union meeting, people might suggest, for example, the divisional council, the NEC and the union's sponsored MPs. There may be restrictions in your group's rules about where they can send letters – many union rules do not allow you to circulate them to other branches, for instance, and the chair or secretary should check on this. There is a tendency in the Labour Party to send motions all over the place, which costs a lot of money and time. It also reduces their impact; if you send motions regularly to people who cannot really deal with them, then when you send them one that is more directly relevant they may take no notice.

One place that groups often do **not** send their resolutions, when they really should, is the local press. If you have agreed a policy or an activity, and you think it worth doing, then surely you will want others to know about it? You could either appoint a press officer, or rotate this task. Look at *Organising Things*, pp. 60–65 (see Further Reading, p. 210) to see how to write and send a press release.

Elections

The annual general meeting of most organizations (see Chapter 6) will involve a large number of elections, but at any other time of the year there may be just one or two elections at a meeting, perhaps because

- someone has resigned from a post;
- you have affiliated to a new group and want to elect someone to go to their meetings;

- your branch has grown in size and you are entitled to another person;
- simply because it is the right time of the year for the other organization; maybe their conference is coming up.

In any case, usually the secretary will have had a letter saying that a delegate is needed, and s/he is responsible for putting it on the agenda.

If there is a conference or an organization to which a member thinks the group should send a delegate – or perhaps in fact s/he is keen to be that delegate – s/he should contact the secretary in advance with details about it and ask him/her to put it on the agenda.

Unless there is an urgent reason for it, no election ought to happen without people being given notice that it is coming up, so that they have the chance to decide if they want to stand, or get someone else to.

Date of next meeting

This is on the agenda to make sure you decide when to have your next meeting before you finish this one. Sometimes this item takes the longest of all; everyone gets out their diaries and shows off about how busy they are and how many other meetings they have on whatever night is suggested. The secretary might be able to work out a few dates in advance. It's almost impossible to find a date all the busy people can agree with. At least the people who are really important for any particular discussion should be able to be there, and all those on one side of a particular argument should not be excluded because they're somewhere else.

Unfortunately, many groups, especially the more informal left ones, and women's groups, assume that everyone knows the date of the next meeting because they were at the last; if you weren't you don't get to hear about the next one until very shortly before it happens, if at all. There are several ways you can deal with this.

- Fix several dates in advance at once and send a letter to all your supporters asking them to put these in their diaries;
- fix the date of each meeting at the end of the last, but send out a letter, or a copy of the minutes, with the date of the next meeting clearly emphasized, as soon as possible afterwards;
- fix a regular date, time and place, like 7.30 on the third Thursday of the month at the church hall, and make sure you tell everyone, especially new members, about it (you will still need to send out an agenda a few days before).

If one of the officers can't be at the meeting, or if you are rotating the jobs (see pp. 64–5), then this is the point at which to decide who is taking them on next time, so that you do not have delays and difficulties at the beginning of the next meeting.

Any other business

This is often referred to as AOB, and appears on most agendas. Sometimes the order of this and date of next meeting is reversed – it does not really matter.

Used properly, this is the place where the odd little bits and pieces, announcements about next week's jumble sale, or a conference one or two people might like to attend, are covered. Anything major should be an item in its own right. However, this often does not happen, and big issues are raised just as everyone is packing up to go home. Sometimes this is because there has been no place for these items anywhere else in the meeting, but sometimes it is deliberate, because people want to get their own way and so they stay behind after other people have left.

One procedure that ensures that everyone knows what is going to come up is for the chair, right at the beginning of the meeting, to ask what items people want to talk about under any other business, and make a note of them, not allowing any other subject to be raised later. This can be seen as rather dictatorial, however, and without a firm chair the meeting can drift into discussing the items there and then, while they are being listed, rather than waiting till later. The chair will need to explain carefully his/her reasons for doing this.

Some groups call this item 'any other competent business'. This simply means that only items about which you do not have to give advance notice under the group's standing orders (see p. 39) can be raised.

One alternative is to have a break just before any other business. Perhaps you can provide a cup of coffee or a glass of wine, let people stretch their legs or look at the bookstall, then return after five minutes, in a more informal way, to hear about the odd bits and pieces and exchange information. Doing this also makes it clear that this slot is not to be used for major items.

Meeting review

Many groups now add another item to their agenda at the end. This is a 'review' of how the meeting has gone. They ask themselves questions like:

- Did we organize our discussion properly, or did we ramble on?

- Did we take clear decisions?
- Did we spend longer than we needed on minor items?

If you're a fairly new group, this can be a good way of learning more about how to run meetings, and it can also give the person who is going to be chair next time a little more confidence. The danger, however, is that if what went wrong was that everyone rambled on about things that didn't matter, they will carry on doing so during this session. You might want to have a review every second or third meeting, and really work on it, rather than let it become part of a routine.

At the end

If there is a time limit on the use of the hall, as there often is, try to stick to it, since it could well involve the caretaker doing extra overtime, or a volunteer staying up late, if you don't. It helps if you announce this at the meeting.

If the group itself is responsible for locking up, someone will have to go round and check the lights are off, and so on.

Afterwards

On p. 79, it is said that how well a meeting went often reflects the amount of work that is put in beforehand. It also involves work afterwards. The secretary – or possibly several people dividing up the job between them – must:

- write up the minutes and circulate them;
- write any letters s/he was asked to;
- send in resolutions, delegation forms for conferences, and so on;
- remind people who did not attend that they may lose their seats unless they turn up soon.

Many unions, and some other groups, issue small handbooks or information sheets to their branch secretaries about what they should do. It's worth asking your head office whether yours does, as it will tell you about any peculiarities your group may have.

Minutes

The appearance, and the length, of the minutes of different groups can vary considerably. Some groups have extremely brief notes, while others are much longer. To be any use, the minutes must say what decisions are taken, but whether they also try to explain why, and what discussions went on, is really a matter of the style decided on. The TUC, for instance, has sets of minutes many pages long, which start by summarizing the paper the committee considered and then give the arguments used by different people before finally saying what was agreed.

Other groups, however, simply say what the point was that was agreed, give the figures for the voting, and leave it at that.

Here are some rules of thumb for writing minutes:

- They need to say clearly **what** was agreed, **and who** is going to carry it out. So, returning to p. 98, where it was agreed that Fred and Mary should take the banner to the demonstration on Sunday, these are the crucial points to enter in the minutes. Some secretaries rule a column down one side of the page and head it 'Action'; under this they write the names of people who've agreed to do a particular job.
- However, if someone was not at your meeting, they might not know what the demonstration is about, and wonder why the group is supporting it anyway. The second important point, therefore, is to make the minutes, together with the other papers that are sent to the group's members, understandable by the people who weren't there.

  To take a different example, at the monthly management committee of the local resource centre, the workers are supposed to report on what they have been doing. The idea is that written reports are sent out in advance, but this doesn't always happen. The person taking the minutes does not need to make detailed notes about the reports that have been sent out in advance, because people have them to read. Any reports that are given verbally, however, do need to be noted down, so that people know what was said. If there are papers that were not sent out in advance, but handed round at the meeting, either send these out along with the minutes, or summarize them in the notes. Even in the papers people have seen, it is useful to jog their memories by saying, in just a few words, what the item was about. So, rather than writing 'Paper 5(9) was discussed and agreed', you could put, 'Paper 5(9) about buying a new minibus was . . .'
- Anyone summarizing a discussion needs to guard against his/her own bias, and make sure that their own views on the subject, which will inevitably creep in to some extent, do not colour the report too much. It is fairly easy to cut out the obvious bias, like describing some opponent's views as

ridiculous, but much more difficult to be sure you've given sufficient space to the other side and not understated their strong points. It could be useful to pass a copy of the minutes, while they are still a draft, to someone who took a different view from you, and ask if s/he thinks them fair.

- If there have been formal resolutions, then everyone needs to know what was decided, by seeing the full text. This can be complicated if there was a series of amendments, but if the secretary is not clear what has been decided, it is unlikely that anyone else will be. The minutes should say which resolutions and amendments were proposed, which ones were passed, and which were not. It is usual to put in the voting figures also, or to say that the resolution was passed 'overwhelmingly', '*nem. con.*' or 'unanimously' (see p. 47).

Start the minutes by giving the date of the meeting that they are about, and a list of who attended, unless there were too many people for this. Then carry on through each item on the agenda, saying what happened and was decided. The example here uses the sort of wording that appears in most sets of minutes, but you do not have to keep to this. So long as it is clear, the language need not be formal. On p. 86 there was an example of the agenda of a meeting and below are the imaginary minutes of the same meeting.

Start off by saying who was there. Some groups list everyone who attends. Others list only officers, and then the number of members. So the first section could read

Minutes of meeting of Cleobury Branch held on Thursday 12 October
Attendance: Cheryl Bloggs (Chair), Tony Odie (Secretary), J. Askham, M. Dixon, D. Evans
or
Attendance: Cheryl Bloggs (Chair), Tony Odie (Secretary) and three other members.

Next come **apologies**. Some groups only list the names, others give the reason as well, like this:

1. **Apologies for Absence** were received from F. Iqbal (union business), T. Gloucester (illness), M Hourani (childcare problems).

You then take the items in the order in which they were dealt with. If the discussion tended to leap from subject to subject, it's legitimate to tidy it up by putting all the points relating to one subject together, even if they occurred at different times during the meeting. If you are doing this a lot add a note to say so, to help people understand what is being done. So the next section says:

2. **The minutes of the last meeting**, which had been previously circulated, were agreed as a correct record, with the amendment of '£500' to '£50' under item 4(a).

Next comes:

3. **Matters arising from the minutes**
(a) Lobby of council. H. Smith reported that this had been arranged for Wednesday 19 October at 7 p.m. He asked all branch members to attend. This was noted.
It was moved by J. Askham, seconded by M. Dixon, that the branch banner be taken along. This was agreed by 15 votes to 8. Fred Jones and Mary Ellis agreed to be responsible for it, and the Secretary agreed to hand it over after the meeting.
(b) Fund-raising social. It was agreed to discuss this item next time, as the fund-raising committee had not yet met.
4. **Correspondence**
The Secretary reported that the following letters had been received, and it was agreed that action should be taken as listed:
(a) Party leader rally – circulate to members.
(b) GLC list of candidates – raise at next branch meeting.

An alternative way to deal with this could be to circulate the correspondence list with the minutes, suitably altered if the decisions were different from the recommendations.

If you took copies of an important letter to hand out at the meeting, you could also attach a copy to the minutes if your resources allow this. The same applies to reports.

5. **Reports**
(a) The executive committee report, previously circulated, was discussed. The recommendations to the GC were dealt with as follows:
(i) It was agreed to buy an Ansaphone for the office.
(ii) It was decided to take no action on the proposal to hold a joint meeting with Minneapolis branch.
(b) Councillor B. Smith gave a verbal report on the council's activities over the last month, especially the privatization of the swimming pools, which Labour had opposed, and gave details of what they had done . . . He was questioned about . . . His report was noted.
(c) Olive Jenkins circulated a written report about Annual Conference (copy attached) and answered questions about it. It

was noted that she had not voted in accordance with Branch policy on abortion. D. Evans proposed a vote of censure, seconded by P. Nailor. After some discussion, R. Hare moved that the meeting move on to next business. This was seconded by L. Harp, and passed by 17 votes to 4.

6. **Talk by Anne Brown**
Ms A. Brown, from the National Executive, spoke about the need to involve more women members in the party, and methods of doing this . . . After a discussion, in which the following points were raised . . . M. Dixon moved a vote of thanks, which was carried unanimously.

Next come the **motions**. If you have had a good many amendments, as in the example on p. 45, you may feel it will be tedious in the extreme to write them all down. It is usual to do so, though, because the minutes are the formal record of what the meeting has done (or decided not to do), and if there is any doubt, you need something to refer back to and settle those doubts. This is how a discussion would look in the minutes.

7. **Motions.** P. Pickard proposed, seconded by R. Lane:
'This meeting supports the strikers and all members agree to donate £5 a week to their hardship fund.'
L. Gran proposed Amendment A, seconded by H. Richard: 'delete £5, insert £1'.
J. Gross proposed Amendment B, seconded L. Bain: 'delete £5, insert £2.50'.
A. Bartlett proposed Amendment C, seconded M. Harvey: 'Insert after strikers "by all possible means including the calling of a general strike in Fenwick-on-Avon on Friday 13 July".'
D. Cole proposed Amendment D, seconded P. Bradley: 'to add after strikers "but considers that this support should be limited to moral and financial help and there should be no call for sympathy strikes".'
After discussion, the Chair ruled that Amendments C and D opposed each other and could not therefore both be passed. Voting was then as follows:
Amendment C: 17 for, 13 against. This was therefore carried, and Amendment D was not taken. Amendment A: 12 for, 8 against. This was therefore carried. Amendment B: 12 for, 14 against. This was therefore lost.

The final part of this minute is the most important. This is where you put down the motion in its final form, called the 'substantive' motion, so that everyone can know exactly what you were left with after all the chopping and changing. So in this case the minute ends:

The substantive motion, reading, 'This meeting supports the strikers by all possible means, including the calling of a general strike in Fenwick-on-Avon on 13 July, and all members agree to donate £1 a week to their hardship fund', was then voted on and carried overwhelmingly. It was agreed to send copies of the resolution to the Trades Council, the National Executive, and the strikers.

8. **Date of Next Meeting**

It was noted that the date of the next meeting had already been fixed, for 11 November, 8 p.m., at the Social Hall.

9. **Any other business**

(a) J. Harris reported that Bilston branch were having a social the following day, and urged members to attend.

(b) R. Higgins brought up the question of the National Executive's action over Liverpool Council, and proposed that a letter should be sent condemning them. The Chair ruled this out of order on the grounds that a resolution should have been put forward earlier in the agenda.

There being no further business, the meeting closed at . . .

Signed ______________________________

Date ______________________________

Although the minutes are not formally agreed until the next meeting, it is sensible for the secretary to check them over with other people, especially the chair, before sending them out. Sometimes in fact chairs insist on this. Double-check any point you are not sure about. Being rude about the minutes, and the secretary, is a habit of some people, usually those who never offer to do the minutes themselves. You can't stop them being rude, but you can reduce their opportunities.

If there has been a personal attack on someone, or people have been making allegations perhaps about someone who wasn't there, take care about what is put in the minutes. You could be libelling them (see p. 198), even though you are only repeating what has already been said. Either leave these comments out altogether or wrap them up with some wording like 'Jeremy Fisher then made comments about P. Jones for which he subsequently agreed to apologize'.

The sooner after the meeting you write the minutes, the easier they will be, because your memory will help you amplify your notes.

If it's within your resources, send copies of the minutes

immediately to anyone who's agreed to do anything, with their names circled in red, little arrows in the margin pointing to them, or some other way of drawing attention to the point they've committed themselves on. This reduces the chances of them forgetting to do what they've agreed to, and certainly reduces their excuses if they fail.

Sending out letters

There are usually several letters to write after a meeting. Letters about resolutions need to say what the resolution is, and what you want done about it. For instance, the letter to the trades council about the branch resolution might say, 'The following resolution was passed at the Cleobury branch meeting [give the resolution]. The branch would be grateful if you could arrange for the Trades Council to discuss it.' The letter to the strikers might say, 'I am sending for your information a note of the resolution that was passed at Cleobury branch, as follows . . .'

If you have elected delegates to any organization, you will have to inform that organization. You may have a form to fill in, and you may also have to send a cheque, which you would get from the treasurer. If there is any delay in this, send off your letter and tell them the cheque will follow. That will usually satisfy them for a few days.

For any other letters, try to tackle them after you have written the minutes, as you will often be able to use the same wording as in the minutes, or to adapt it slightly. If you keep closely to the minutes, you will avoid accusations that you are not conveying what was decided at the meeting. You need to be aware of the danger of letting your own bias creep in.

Keep copies of the letters you send. You might find it useful also to make a list of the ones to which you are expecting a reply, so that you can send reminders, or telephone, if you haven't heard anything before the next meeting.

There could be a good deal of other follow-up work, putting the decisions of the group into practice. This is not dealt with in this book, however, as it covers a lot more than simply running a meeting. Look at *Organising Things* (see Further Reading p. 210) for ideas on how to set about running events, such as marches, festivals and public meetings.

5.

Alternative practice for meetings

The last chapter looked at conventional ways of running meetings and some variations to make them more interesting, so if you are thinking about how to run your own group, it may be useful for you to refer back.

This chapter considers the different ways in which a group that wants to be informal and non-hierarchical might operate, based on the ideas outlined and developed in Chapter 3.

There are two principles behind the suggestions here. These are:

- that no one person has special power in the group, or extra knowledge;
- that every effort is made to **involve** all those who attend the group's meetings in its discussions and activities.

Chairing

On p. 64 ways are suggested of rotating the jobs among the group. At the meeting itself, the most important job is that of chair, and people used to conventional meetings are often very sceptical of the idea that 'just anyone' can be chair. It is a job that can be quite arduous, and is something that frightens many people. This is one reason why those who are less sensitive tend to monopolize the job. When you suggest that there should be a different chair for every meeting, people are likely to say, 'But some of our members couldn't possibly do it, they wouldn't know how,' or 'But they would be too weak, they would let X monopolize the meeting.'

There are several answers to this:

- If changing the way we run meetings is about spreading the power out, as is suggested on p. 63, then the chair, in whom much of the power is based, has got to have that power taken away.
- Many people who chair all sorts of meetings are not particularly good at it anyway, simply confident. Therefore it is not a

question of replacing brilliant people with idiots, but of shifting between several more or less competent people.

- Inexperienced people may make a mess of chairing to start with, but the best way to learn is through experience, and people do learn very quickly. If chairing your meeting is an absolute nightmare, with factions throwing the tables around, then something is seriously wrong, and just shifting round the officers will not remove the problem; you need to examine what is really going on, and see how it can be put right.

In any case, if the job is rotated among the members, so that everyone has a turn sooner or later, they should all get to appreciate the difficulties and be more tolerant.

That may be wishful thinking in some cases, as one cannot deny that some people can be very difficult. The most difficult may be those who think that the idea of rotating the chair is absurd, and are out to prove it by creating problems for the different chairs. For this reason, it's not wise to embark on the experiment of taking turns unless there is considerable support for it. Without this, it could be a disaster and undermine people's self-confidence.

Even chairing a formally run meeting is not that difficult, so long as you have time beforehand to check up on the various procedures. Informal meetings are usually easier, although it still takes concentration and confidence. A general idea of the role a chairperson must fulfil is given on p. 97.

Greater involvement

One reason that in conventional meetings a small group manages to retain power is that they are the ones who talk most, because they hang on to the things to talk about. The chair and secretary, in particular, read the letters, give the reports from other meetings and tell people about the various matters arising. There's no way in which you can stop some people knowing more than others, or talking more than others, but you can spread out the work of telling the meeting what is going on. This can happen even when the official responsibilities have to stay with a few people on account of your group's rules.

So, for example, the secretary may still be sent all letters, but a different person at each meeting could take the bundle of letters and read them out, or summarize them, while the person taking notes does only that job – which will make the job easier for him/her, too. If there is a report to be given from a meeting or conference, those who have attended it could split between them the task of talking about it.

It will help if they put the report in writing and simply answer questions about it, as was suggested on p. 104.

At the beginning of a meeting, when you're looking at the list of points to discuss (see p. 100), try to arrange for different people to start off the discussion on each item. People will feel shy about doing this at first, but if everyone participates, it will not seem so difficult for any one person.

The more you rotate the jobs, the more careful you will need to be about the **information** that is passed on with each one, otherwise there will be chaos. Perhaps the best way is to have a set of files or plastic wallets with the necessary information in each. You could have one for the membership secretary, one for the person taking the minutes and one for the chair. So, for example, for the person with the responsibility for telling people after each meeting when and where the next one is to be, you could have ready:

- an up-to-date membership list, or perhaps a set of labels printed on someone's computer;
- information about where to get anything photocopied or duplicated;
- examples of the letters sent out previously.

In another file, you could also assemble the bits of paper relating to booking the room, getting hold of the bookstall, and so on.

You also must be sure that everyone knows how to get in touch with each other in case of difficulties. So there should be a list of telephone numbers in the front of each file. And, as suggested on p. 77, the arrangements for paying back any expenses incurred should be spelt out. If postage is going to be a large amount, as it is for some groups, then either the treasurer could get a large stock of stamps and they could be included in the file, or the secretary for that month could be asked to buy stamps and claim the money back, with a receipt from the Post Office.

How people talk

Appendix 1, on pp. 201–4, is a list of words and phrases used at formal meetings. From it, and from the first part of the book, you can see how far a special language has developed. Some of it is old-fashioned, some is a jargon that has been created, perhaps to make the meeting remote from what goes on in the world outside. It is another way in which power is given to those who know how to talk that way.

One therefore must put considerable effort into changing the way people talk and stressing the need to use ordinary words, with their ordinary meanings, not jargon or initials.

This involves the chair, and other members as well, listening hard to what people say and breaking in and asking for an explanation whenever jargon is used. The use of initials is a problem. Organizations like the Labour Party have all sorts of committees and conferences with long names, and to use the full name each time is rather cumbersome. It may not be possible to ban initials all the time, but to make sure that the **first** time someone says GC or NEC they explain that it means general committee or national executive committee.

You could have a blackboard or large sheet of paper on the wall on which people have to write the meaning of any set of initials the first time it is used, so that everyone can see what is being referred to. Some groups have circulated a list of set initials to all their members. This though has the disadvantage that it makes them into more, rather than less, of an institution; people feel licensed to use them as much as they want.

One possibility of stopping people using jargon is to have a 'jargon chart'. This is a large sheet of paper stuck on the wall, or a blackboard, on which the chair writes up any word that someone has used and another member does not understand. At a convenient point during the meeting, the person who used the word has to explain it.

This idea was developed by the TUC Training College, because they found it a good way of ensuring that people did not talk over others' heads, and also because it tends to deflate the egos of self-important shop stewards and union officials (almost always men) who use long words to impress, without quite knowing what they mean. Seeing that sort of person flounder can give a boost to the confidence of everyone else, who may have been feeling put down.

If you are in an established group that's changing its ways, it's often quite difficult to clear away the special language, because those who know it will not recognize how odd it really is. Much of it involves ordinary words used in strange, shorthand constructions. 'Move the vote be put,' for instance, does not actually make sense, although you might be able to work out that it means, 'I suggest that we now vote on this.' It is a hard, continuous slog checking people and asking them to translate, and they often get quite upset or irritated. For this reason not just the chair but the other members should be prepared to do this.

Preparation and follow-up

If a meeting is going to be worthwhile, people are going to need to think about it both before, and afterwards, preparing for it and following up the decisions that were taken. In a formal organization, most of the work falls on the secretary, with the chair assisting a little, as explained on p. 111. This means s/he has considerable power, as well as considerable responsibility. The alternative is to allocate various tasks to people as the decisions are made. You then need someone to co-ordinate, as well as jog people's memories about what they agreed to do. If you are rotating the jobs, the person who types the minutes of a particular meeting could have the task of 'progress chasing' between that meeting and the next. If you have permanent jobs, you could split this role from that of the secretary and call it 'co-ordinator'.

It can be helpful, if you are arranging something complicated, perhaps a large event like a festival, to have a pyramid structure so that a lot of people have specific responsibilities, but so that they channel information through two or three 'co-ordinators', specializing in different aspects. This means that if the individual cannot get to a specific meeting, there is someone else there who also knows about the subject.

However, this can develop into a rather rigid hierarchy, and you need to take care to keep the balance between co-ordination and authority.

It is part of the character of a group organized informally that it needs to trust its members to do what they said they would. There are bound to be occasional slip-ups and let-downs, and those who don't like this way of working will use these as a reason for returning to the old ways. However, the formal structure is just as prone to slip-ups. Since so much work is piled on to one or two people, the chances that something will get lost, or fail to be done, are, if anything, greater.

6.

Annual general meetings

Every group that is formally constituted – and many that are not – will have an annual general meeting (AGM) each year. This chapter explains how to set about it. It is written for the group with fixed, rather than rotating, tasks. A less formally run group would want to divide up the jobs among all its members, but the jobs would still need to be done.

The purpose of the annual general meeting is to report to the members about what the organization has been doing in the last year and to elect new officers. The constitutional role of the AGM is explained on p. 25. This chapter explains how an AGM is run, and what procedure is used, as it will not always be the same as for an ordinary meeting.

The official role of the AGM is for the ordinary members to find out what their organization is doing, to say whether they like it or not, and to change it if they do not. The management committee report to the members, who decide what their policy should be. An organization that has a number of levels will usually have an annual general meeting at each level. So in the Labour Party, for example, each branch has an AGM. This elects the officers of the branch, and also the delegates (see p. 25) to the general committee (GC). This GC then itself has an AGM, to which all these delegates are invited. They elect the officers, the executive committee, and the delegates to the District Party. The District Party itself then has its AGM and elects its own officers. In addition, the GC at some point in the year will elect delegates to the Regional Conference, and the National Conference, which are the AGMs of the regional and national levels of the party respectively.

AGMs vary considerably in importance between groups. For some, they are a five-minute formality, whereas for others they are a key part of the calendar. This chapter assumes the AGM is quite important.

Preparations

The rules of many organizations tell you the month in which you have to hold the AGM. If they do not, there may be a custom that people have always followed. Legally, you need to have one AGM in each calendar year, if you are a limited company or a charity, but you may have discretion to let it slip a little if necessary, perhaps so that the meeting is 15 months after the last one.

It is the secretary's responsibility to call the AGM. S/he needs to start thinking about it well in advance, because there are often a number of detailed preparations to make. Put on the agenda of an ordinary meeting at least two months earlier an item about 'preparation for the AGM' and ask people to decide about setting a date and booking a room. You may have more people coming to the AGM than to an ordinary meeting – is the usual room going to be big enough? Try to make sure that there is somewhere else, even if only a kitchen, where the votes can be counted while the meeting is going on. You could arrange refreshments, and make it an occasion where people can talk informally about the group and meet the staff in a different atmosphere from the usual one. You could also have an exhibition or display of the work you do. An AGM can be – and should be – the occasion for propaganda among users and the public.

All those entitled to come will need to be told about the AGM well in advance. Usually the constitution gives a minimum time, often three weeks, even though for an ordinary meeting it may be only a week. For a company, it must be three weeks' notice by law.

All members must be notified, as well as trustees, if you have any. If you are an organization that notifies all the members about the meetings anyway, like a trade-union branch, this will be no problem; but if a committee runs your business for the rest of the year, people may need to spend some time getting membership records straight and checking who has paid up and who has not. This would usually be the job of the treasurer and/or the membership secretary, who should give the secretary an up-to-date list in time for the invitations to the AGM to be sent out.

Think also about any celebrities, special guests, or press you want to invite.

Annual report

Many constitutions say you **must** produce an annual report, although they may not specify the length or the form it should take. The officers and committee need to give a report to the meeting. Usually this will be in writing, though not always.

Some organizations, especially voluntary groups, prepare a brochure, which can be used later for fund-raising and publicity. Others produce a few duplicated sheets, or include a brief report in their newsletter or magazine. In others, the chair simply says a few words, perhaps followed by the secretary and the treasurer.

Preparing a written report to send out in advance is an arduous chore and is not necessary for a small informal organization, but for the larger one it does have several advantages.

- It makes the officers and committee think about what they actually have done, and whether it was worth doing. If they are scratching around for things to report, it may make a sleepy committee realize that they have not been very constructive over the last year and that they will have to pull their socks up if they are not to get into trouble with the members.
- It gives the members a chance to digest the report, to think about their criticisms, and perhaps to get together to work out how to get things changed. This, of course, is why a sleepy committee, or one that is not keen to share power, may try not to report to the members in advance, since that will make it more difficult to organize any opposition.
- It means that people who can't get to the meeting are still kept in touch with what is going on.
- It gives you an opportunity to promote the organization, tell people what good work you're doing, and perhaps recruit new members.

If the group is going to produce a detailed report, plan this well in advance. Ask each person who has a specific task (the secretary, the membership secretary, any paid workers), to write a brief piece, and delegate one person – the chair, if you have one – to write an introduction. Then one person, or a small group, should edit it into a consistent style, decide on any pictures and what sort of design you are going to have. They, or another person, then should be responsible for its **production**, whether this means getting it to the printer or sweating over a duplicator (look at *Organising Things*, Chapter 4 see Further Reading, p. 210) for details on production methods). Finally, they will have to arrange its distribution.

If it is not possible to get a report together in advance of the meeting, then those who can't attend should be told that copies of what is handed out at the meeting will be available if they contact the secretary.

Treasurer's report and accounts

These will usually be incorporated in the annual report at the back. However, even if you are having a verbal presentation for the other officers, the treasurer's report and accounts must be in writing.

Almost every constitution says that the accounts must be presented to the AGM, and very often they have to be audited (see p. 29). It is often difficult to get the accounts ready in time for the AGM, especially if the year they cover has only just ended, but it is important. If there are continuing difficulties with this, you could change the financial year to fit in better with the AGM, or vice versa.

Advance information

Generally there should be two mailings before the AGM. The first should give notice, and ask for nominations. The second will include the agenda, the annual report and the list of nominations. The papers that need to be prepared and either sent out in advance or circulated at the meeting, are:

- formal notice of the meeting;
- request for nominations;
- list of existing officers, and how many meetings they have been to (this is called the 'attendance record');
- the minutes of the last AGM;
- the annual report;
- the accounts;
- list of people who have been nominated and perhaps details about them;
- ballot papers if you have a postal ballot;
- the agenda for the meeting.

The time at which these must go out may be laid down in the constitution. For instance, the agenda may have to be sent out 'not less than 21 days' in advance. It will be important to keep to these limits, or you could find the whole procedure is legally invalid (see Chapter 10).

Formal notice

This may be combined with the **agenda**, or it may be on its own. It is often in the form of a letter, and it could also include the request for nominations. The points it must include are the time, date and place of the meeting, and the fact that elections are going to take place and reports to be presented. In order for the AGM to be valid, these points **have** to be included. The notice must be brought to the attention of all the members, either by sending it to them, or by pinning it on a notice board where everyone can see it.

Request for nominations

People will have to be asked to nominate for all the jobs that are up for election. Usually all the officers and the committee are elected each year, although occasionally their term of office will be longer. You may also need to elect auditors (see p. 29) and perhaps also delegates to other groups with whom you have links, or a district or area committee of your organization. The constitution should list all these jobs, but check also last year's AGM agenda to make sure you have not missed anyone. It's useful to add to this the list of current office holders, and the numbers of meetings they've attended, compared to the number they should have been at.

The constitution should also say whether nominations have to be in by a certain date, perhaps seven days before the meeting. Once this date is passed, the secretary may have to circulate a list of the nominations to the members before the meeting. There is usually also a procedure for taking names 'from the floor', that is, at the meeting itself, if too few people are put forward in advance.

Very often, there are fewer nominations than places. People are particularly unenthusiastic about taking on the jobs that involve doing some bureaucratic work, such as being secretary. If the officers or committee members want to drop out, or if people do not think they are very good and want a change, there will have to be some arm-twisting well in advance. If it is permitted under the constitution, this might be the time to suggest splitting some tasks to spread the load, doing away with unnecessary posts, and rotating others around the organization, as explained in Chapter 3.

The question of what details you should ask people to give if they are standing for elections, and whether they should address the meeting, is discussed on p. 130.

Minutes of the last AGM

It may seem odd to resurrect these, since they record what happened last year. The point is that the AGM follows on from that last one, not from the ordinary meetings, because a different group of people will come to it. So only one AGM can approve the minutes of another. This can be a formality, because people will not be able to remember what happened last year to tell you whether the minutes are accurate or not. They are intended also to remind you about what happened last year. Were there promises made about things to be done, and have they been carried out? Were particular problems highlighted and have they been solved? It is another way, like the annual report already covered on p. 125, of assessing your managing committee's performance and seeing if it is doing a useful job.

Agenda

This tends to look much the same from year to year, as people will carefully copy the previous year's agenda to ensure that they have left nothing out. Here is an example of the agenda for Anytown Labour Party's AGM.

1. Apologies.
2. Minutes of the 1984 AGM and matters arising.
3. Election of Tellers.
4. Election of officers (a) Chairperson
   (b) Vice-Chair
   (c) Secretary
   (d) Treasurer
   (e) Social Secretary.
5. Consideration of Annual Report.
6. Consideration of Secretary's Report.
7. Consideration of Treasurer's Report.
8. Election of Executive Committee.
9. Election of Schools Subcommittee.
10. Election of 2 conference delegates.
11. Election of 2 auditors for the coming year.
12. Any other business.

As you can see, it is rather long and boring, and most of the time will be taken up with formal reports and elections. It can be made slightly more interesting by taking the reports and any motions or other business in the intervals between the elections, while you are waiting for the votes to be counted, rather than at the end. If you are doing this, warn people, when the notice goes out, that items will not necessarily be covered in the order in which they are listed.

In the same notice, people should be told what the procedure is for voting and also warned if, for instance, their membership cards are to be checked and only those who are fully paid up are allowed in. So Anytown Labour Party would put on the bottom of their agenda:

1. Items will be taken in sequence as far as possible while the various elections are in progress, but the consideration of reports, etc., will be taken out of order to avoid unnecessary delay.

2. Where an election is contested by more than two people, the election will be by exhaustive ballot. Elections will all be by secret ballot.

3. Members' cards will be checked on the door and only those who are up to date with their subscriptions will be admitted.

At the meeting

At or near the beginning of the AGM you will need to appoint the **tellers**. Their function was explained on p. 47. The job is much more important at this meeting than at others, because of the number of elections, and so people may be all the more reluctant to take on the responsibility. One possible source of volunteers is smokers, if the meeting has voted to ban smoking, as the tellers can have a cigarette while counting in another room.

Having had the reports from the officers and committee put forward and discussed the next thing will be the elections. These could be for the whole management or executive committee, who then elect their own officers at their first meeting. More usually, the chair will be the first one to be elected. If the current person is standing for re-election, it could be difficult for him/her to act fairly during the election, so usually the existing secretary or vice-chair takes over until this election is finished.

Elections

These can take place at the meeting itself, or there may be a postal ballot in advance, the results of which are declared at the meeting, or these two methods are combined.

However it is done, formally a person needs a **proposer**, who first puts his/her name forward, and a seconder, who backs it up. See p. 13 for an example of this. You also need the agreement of the person concerned. Many groups send out a form that incorporates all this. Below is an example from Gateway Community Centre.

Nomination form for Management Committee of Gateway Community Centre. To be returned to the Centre by 20 November 1985.

I ____

of ____

being a registered member of the Gateway Community Centre, hereby nominate ______________________________ of ____

for the position of __________ (insert Chair, Treasurer, Secretary, Member as appropriate) on the Management Committee of Gateway Community Centre from November 1985 to November 1986.

Proposer: Signed ______________________________

Seconder: Signed ______________________________

I agree to my nomination

Signed ______________________________

If you are having a **postal ballot** you will need to allow time to send out the ballot forms and for them to be returned. Usually the closing date for the ballot would be the date of the meeting itself, so that people can bring their papers with them. You then count the votes during the meeting and announce the result at the end. If this is too difficult, set the closing date a few days in advance so there is time to do the counting at more leisure.

Do you want the postal ballot to be secret? If so, each person needs to be sent two envelopes. The first, inner, one should be marked 'ballot paper only'. The ballot paper goes in this, and nothing else. It is then sealed up, and put into the other one, on which the member writes his/her name, and address or membership number. The people counting up then take all the envelopes, check the names, addresses and membership numbers on a list, and then open and discard (or put in a separate place, in case there is a later query) all the outer envelopes. Only then do they open the inner ones, so they cannot tell which paper comes from which person.

You will also need to decide what **form** of voting you are using – the various types are explained below – and write a clear explanation to send out with the papers. If it is not clear, you get a lot of wasted votes, so it is worth taking trouble about it.

When nominations are taken at the meeting from the floor, the chair will start by asking, 'Are there any nominations?' and then someone will say, 'I nominate Martha Biggs,' someone else will say, 'I second that,' or 'Seconded,' and other people will suggest other names. You are not supposed to nominate yourself, but you can always ask someone in advance to do it, or prod them during the meeting and whisper your request.

After a few names have been given, someone may say, 'Move nominations close,' (or 'cease'), meaning, 'I suggest we stop nominating people.' Each candidate may then be asked to say a few words about why s/he thinks they would be the best person for the job, or about political views, and then you vote between the candidates. If there are only two people standing, you simply vote for one or the other. If there are several people, and perhaps also several jobs, it becomes more difficult. There are several different voting systems, but the main ones are:

- first past the post. This is the method used in council and parliamentary elections in Britain. You have the same number of votes as there are places to fill, although you don't usually have to use them all. There is only one ballot and the people with the highest number of votes are elected. This is often felt to be very unfair, because there may be a lot more people voting against the winner than for him/her, but the anti-vote may be split between several people. Some groups use a variation of this, modelled on the French system, where the two people who come top in the first ballot have a 'run-off' between them. That is, you vote a second time just between those two, everyone else having dropped out.
- alternative voting. This has a number of variations, such as single transferable vote. Get the organization using them to explain the details. The basic method is that on the ballot paper you number your preferences, that is, you put who you like the best, second best, and so on. So you might put Smith first, Jones second and Brown third.

  If any candidate gets more than half the first preferences of voters on the first ballot, s/he is elected. If not, the person with the **lowest** number of first preferences is eliminated, and the ballot papers are counted again, with the second preferences of the people who voted for the eliminated person re-allocated.

  So if, having put Smith first, s/he drops out, on the second round your vote goes to Jones, who was second on the list. This process goes on, with the bottom candidate dropping out each time, until the top candidate has an overall majority.
- exhaustive ballot. This is the method used in electing candidates for council or parliamentary elections. The standard joke is that it's an exhaust*ing* ballot, because if there are several candidates it can take hours.

  You have a ballot paper on which you mark down your votes for however many places there are. If you're electing a parliamentary candidate, you'd have only one vote because there's only one place. If you're electing an executive committee you might have six places to fill, and therefore six votes. The **tellers** or the **scrutineers** (see p. 47) then count the votes and the result is announced. The person with the lowest number of votes is then **eliminated**, which means s/he drops out, so that you can't vote for him/her any more, and you vote again between those who are left. So if you voted for the person who has dropped out, you have to give your vote this time to someone else. This process is then repeated until only the right number of people for the places vacant are left.

Usually you **must** vote for the right number of people if you vote at all; so if there are six places you have to use your six votes, even if there are only three people you really like the look of.

If two people's votes added together come to less than the total vote of the next person, they are **both** eliminated. So if Jones gets three votes, Smith gets five, and Brown gets nine, then Smith and Jones both drop out.

If two or more people tie for bottom place, there's a separate vote, called a **run-off**, between the two, and the person with fewer votes in this drops out.

Citrine and Hannington (see p. 37) both describe an even longer process for exhaustive balloting, where you vote each time for one fewer than the number of candidates left, but this is not used these days.

There are other, even more complicated, voting methods around, but these should be explained before the process starts. If you don't understand the voting system being used in your organization, ask for it to be explained. The chances are that half the rest of the room don't understand either and will heave a sigh of relief that someone's had the nerve to say so.

'Slates'

Often, especially in a big organization or one that has several political factions fighting it out, people will get together beforehand and decide on a list of people to vote for. This is usually called a 'slate'. There may be a left-wing slate and a right-wing slate, and perhaps also a third 'moderate' slate in between.

In some organizations these are against the rules, or frowned on, and then the lists will be passed round secretly, or people may whisper to each other. In other cases, it is done quite openly. Where there are organized slates, a person who is not on anyone's list probably won't get elected. On the other hand, someone who manages to get on both lists, as canny people do at times, will almost certainly be elected, so you could afford to use your vote then for someone else you wanted.

Tactical voting

This is where you vote for someone you don't really like to improve the chances of someone you do like or spoil the chances of someone you like even less. For instance, on an exhaustive ballot (see above) a group of people might vote for Smith on the first round to try to make sure that Jones gets fewer votes and comes out bottom. In the next round, they would take all their votes away from Smith, whom they didn't really like, and start voting for people they really do support.

These tactics can become very complicated and subtle. Some people find them fascinating, and become real experts; they may go into huddles in the corner all the time, to plot what to do, and then give lengthy explanations in the pub afterwards about why it worked or didn't work. For them it's a hobby, like train-spotting. For others, it's a bore, and the easiest thing to do is then to find someone who **is** interested, and whom you trust, and follow their advice.

Afterwards

In some organizations, particularly smaller groups, the new chair or secretary takes over at that meeting, as soon as they have been elected. In others, the old officers carry on until the end of the meeting and then change over. There is no hard-and-fast rule about it, so follow whichever custom has grown up in your organization.

After the AGM itself, someone, usually the secretary, will need to follow through the decisions that have been made.

- Your national or district headquarters may need notifying of the names and addresses of new officers.
- Groups to whom you are sending delegates will need to know who your new delegates are.
- You may have to send the accounts, and/or the annual report, to anyone who has given you grants, to the Charity Commissioners, or to your head office.
- The **minutes** technically are not needed until next year's AGM, but if you leave them until then, you probably won't be able to make anything of your notes. It's better to write them up immediately, while things are fresh, and then keep them safe until next year. You might want to circulate copies of them, stressing that they are for information only, before your next meeting, or you could, alternatively, put the decisions, and the list of new officers and committee, into an information sheet for the members.

If there are new members on the committee, they need to know how it works. Someone – a paid worker if they exist, or the old secretary – should be responsible for briefing them. The information a new member needs is:

- when and where the meetings are;
- how long they last;
- whether expenses are paid, including childcare expenses (as they should be);
- how far in advance the papers are sent out.

In addition, they need to know about the existing policies of the group, if they are not already involved. Some groups send copies of past sets of minutes and papers, at least those that are relevant to current discussions, to all new members. Others also make a point of inviting the new members to tour the office or centre, giving them a chance to meet the staff and the users. Both are good ideas. Another is to arrange for the new officers to meet up with the old ones, to discuss what happens at the meetings. This would not be possible, though, in cases where one organized group had defeated another and relations were bad all round.

As a new officer, hang on to the papers from past committees. This is for practical reasons, as you may need to look back to find out what decision was taken some years ago, especially if you get into some dispute. Also, your old papers will be useful to future historians. If you don't want to keep them yourself, send them to your head office, or hand them over to the local history section of your library.

Checklist

Constitution, rules or standing orders

clause in your rules

What time of year is your AGM? (p. 124) ____________
How much notice has to be given? (p. 126) ____________
When do the other papers have to be sent out? (p. 126) ____________
What business is done there? (pp. 125–6) ____________
Are there resolutions? ____________
Are the elections held at the meetings? (p. 129) ____________
Do the committee have to present a report? Should it be written, or verbal? (p. 126) ____________
Who must be notified? (p. 125) ____________

Arrangements

Have you fixed a date, time and place? (p. 124) ____________
Is there room to count the votes? (p. 124) ____________
Are you having refreshments beforehand, or afterwards? (p. 124) ____________
Who's providing them? (p. 124) ____________
Who's clearing up? (p. 124) ____________
Are you having an exhibition or display of your group's work? (p. 123) ____________
Who's organizing it? (p. 123) ____________
Are you having a crèche? Or paying childcare expenses? (p. 123) ____________
Are you inviting any special guests? (p. 123) ____________
The press? (p. 123) ____________
Have you an up-to-date list of members? (p. 123) ____________

Annual report

What are you putting in it? (pp. 125–6) ____________
Who's writing it? (pp. 125–6) ____________
When must it be ready by? (pp. 125–6) ____________
Who's editing it? (pp. 125–6) ____________
Is it being printed/duplicated/photocopied? (pp. 125–6) ____________
Who are you sending it to? (pp. 125–6) ____________
Is the treasurer's report going to be ready? (p. 126) ____________
Are the accounts ready? (p. 126) ____________

Who's auditing them? (p. 126) ______

How many copies of the report and accounts do you need? (p. 126) ______

Papers to send out

Have you got ready:

formal notice of meeting? (p. 126) ______

request for nominations? (p. 126) ______

list of existing officers? (p. 126) ______

their attendance record? (p. 126) ______

the minutes of the last AGM? (p. 126) ______

the annual report? (p. 126) ______

the accounts? (p. 126) ______

the list of people nominated, and any details? (p. 127) ______

the ballot papers (for a postal ballot)? (p. 130) ______

the agenda for the meeting? (p. 129) ______

What are the deadlines you must keep to, for these? (p. 129) ______

Does the agenda cover everything laid down in the constitution? (p. 129) ______

Are there any other points you need to add? (p. 129) ______

What voting procedure are you using? (p. 131) ______

Have you explained it? (p. 131) ______

At the meeting

Return to the 'arrangements' section for points on the hall, or crèche, the refreshments, exhibition, etc., and check these through again. Is everything still going according to plan? ______

Have you got copies of any papers you need to hand out? (p. 128) ______

If you're voting at the meeting, have you got ballot papers? (p. 130) ______

Have you:

spare copies of all the papers you sent out, for anyone who's lost theirs? (p. 128) ______

a membership list on which to check people's names? (p. 123) ______

Are tellers elected? (p. 129) ______

Where and when are they counting the votes? (p. 129) ______

Who is running the election for chair? (p. 129) ______

Who is taking the notes? (p. 129) ______

Afterwards

Who is sending out the annual report to:
those who didn't attend? (p. 133) ______
funding bodies? (p. 133) ______
the Charity Commission? (p. 133) ______
anyone else interested? (p. 133) ______
What are you sending to the press? (p. 133) ______
Have you notified your headquarters, and anyone else who needs to know, about changes of officers? (p. 133) ______
Have you notified groups to whom you are sending delegates? (p. 133) ______
When is the first management committee meeting? (p. 133) ______
Do the new members know when and where it meets? (p. 133) ______
Have they been sent copies of previous minutes and papers? (p. 133) ______
Have they been invited in to have a look round? (p. 133) ______
Have the old officers and the new had a meeting? (p. 133) ______
Have you put away the old papers somewhere safe? (p. 133) ______

7.

Large conferences

This chapter is about big conferences, for instance that of the Labour Party, trade unions, or pressure groups, and the procedures which they use. It covers both how you get there, and get business discussed, and the procedures that are used at the conference itself. As in the previous chapter on smaller meetings, it is assumed that if you have a choice, you may want to change or reduce the formalities.

However, it is more difficult to make changes here than for smaller meetings, because:

- since the numbers are much larger, keeping people together and making sure they all know what they are doing is more difficult;
- people will have different levels of interest, and different degrees of knowledge about the subject, and also different aims in attending the conference.

If you are introducing changes, or trying to, it is important to define what the aims of the conference are, and make sure your changes do not contradict these aims.

The structure, therefore, needs to be more carefully thought out, and adhered to, than for an ordinary meeting. You also need to take considerable trouble over making it clear what is happening.

The left has not been very successful in changing the ways that conferences are run. Some of the early women's liberation movement conferences, for instance, were chaotic, and since then many people have been put off experimenting with the format. Neither this chapter, nor the next, on running your own conferences, therefore, suggest anything very radical. Rather, it is a matter of trying to make the conventional arrangements a little more friendly.

This chapter is written both for the delegate to a conference and the people organizing it or chairing it. It can only give general guidance, as there are many points where you will need to check your own group's procedures. The various examples used certainly won't apply to every group.

Types of conference

There are two types of large conference in which the labour movement becomes involved today, and they are run in rather different ways:

- decision-making conferences. These are often the annual general meetings (see Chapter 6) of a national organization. They tend to stick to the traditional methods of running conferences outlined in this chapter;
- discussion conferences. There is a traditional way of running these too, but instead they are often run in a way which began as an alternative to the formal arrangements, but which has now become just as standardized and which also has its drawbacks.

This chapter looks at the decision-making type first, then the discussion type.

Attending

For most conferences, it is not necessary actually to be a delegate to get there. You could be a visitor, or an observer, and watch what is going on without taking part. Indeed, if you are just getting involved in your union affairs, for instance, this is a useful thing to do, to get the feel of the organization, before you try to participate actively. However, if you want to take a hand in the decision-making process, you will need to become a delegate. This will mean you have to be elected, or appointed, by a particular group.

The words used vary between groups; this chapter will use the term 'elected', but your rules might talk about being 'nominated', which simply means named, or 'delegated'.

First of all, you need to find out who decides who will attend; when they decide; whether you need any qualifications, for instance, that you have been a member for a specific length of time and have not been in arrears with your contributions.

Look in the rule book, constitution or standing orders. If it is not clear from the rule book, the best person to tell you is usually the secretary, who will have to arrange it all and should know. If, however, you don't want him/her to know you are thinking about trying to become a delegate, or if s/he doesn't seem to know, phone the people who will be doing the donkey work for the conference and ask them. For some organizations, there is a special conference office, but for most there is someone on the administrative staff dealing with it. Delegates to major conferences are often appointed several months before they take place, so find out in good time.

- NUPE's rules, for instance, say that branches with between 250 and 2,000 members are entitled to send one delegate. Branches with over 2,000 members can send an extra delegate. Small branches are grouped together to elect delegates by ballot. All delegates have to be paid-up members of the union, but full-time officers and members of some national committees are not allowed to be delegates. The rule book, however, does not tell you when the election takes place, so you would need to find this out from somewhere else. In fact it is left to the discretion of the branch when to hold the election. In the Labour Party, some branches elect their conference delegates in February, while others leave it until July or August.

You will also have to discover the **procedure** for being elected. Usually you will need to find someone to propose and second you, and you might have to give your consent in writing. Does your name have to be put forward beforehand, perhaps in a letter from the people proposing you, or can it be given at the meeting itself? Will you be asked to speak at the meeting to explain why you want to go, and to answer questions, or will you be asked to put a statement in writing? NUPE's rules, to take the same example, say that the grouped branches 'shall receive with their ballot papers statements indicating their personal qualifications in not more than 200 words, prepared by the candidates'.

There is not always great competition for the job of delegate. If your branch is rather apathetic and takes little interest in national affairs, it may be quite easy to get yourself elected. On the other hand, there may be people who have been going as delegate for years and who want to go again this year. It could then be a hard-fought contest. In these cases, you are unlikely to succeed if you leave it to chance, or luck, on the night of the meeting itself. Someone may need prompting to put your name forward, and you may also need to persuade people that they should vote for you.

It can be very hard to dislodge the sitting member who has been going to the same conference for years, because people feel sorry for him/her and don't like to upset anyone, even if s/he doesn't seem to be doing anything very useful.

Find out what you will actually be allowed to do as a delegate. In some cases, only the delegation's leader, probably a long-established and experienced person, is allowed to speak. S/he might also take the decisions about which way to vote, although more usually you would have a say in it.

Preparations for delegates

Assuming you have had your name put forward, what happens next? You may receive some conference papers fairly soon, possibly a letter saying that you have been appointed, and perhaps the preliminary agenda (see p. 143). If you have heard nothing within a month of your appointment, it might be wise to check with the secretary that everything is in order. However, the bulk of the conference papers probably won't arrive until quite late, and you will probably have to collect some at the conference itself.

Other points to check are:

- when you have to be there. You might have to arrive a day or two before the conference itself, to go to a compositing meeting (see p. 148). Alternatively, you might have to go to another meeting in advance.
- accommodation. Is this arranged for you, or do you have to book a hotel for yourself? Usually if you have to book, they will send you a list of hotels. If not, try ringing up the Information Office or the Tourist Office of the town and ask them for a list.
- meals. If you want to book an evening meal as well as bed and breakfast, check first that it is not going to be served before the conference ends. There are very often 'fringe meetings' immediately after the conference, which you will have to miss if you want to go back to your hotel to eat.
- what happens to your expenses. Sometimes the branch or local organization pays these, sometimes the national organization. In other cases, such as the GMBATU, the costs are shared between the branch and the national office. In other instances it will be assumed that you pay for yourself. This should be opposed; if it is important enough to your organization to send a delegate, they should also pay for that delegate. Otherwise your fellow members are penalizing you for taking on the job of representing them. In other organizations (particularly ones like the Labour Party) they will be willing to pay if anyone asks, but don't actually offer the money. If, however, you need the cash, don't hesitate to ask for it.

  Similarly, if you need an advance on your expenses, to pay the deposit for the hotel or simply to live while you are there, ask for it. Most organizations have or can arrange for facilities for this.
- arrangements for a crèche, if you need one. There is a crèche at most large conferences these days, but not every one. If nothing is provided, make a fuss. But it is only fair also to notify them in

advance that your child will be using it, and what age s/he is.

- other special needs. Are the organizers catering for people with disabilities, or arranging sign language for deaf people? If not, make a fuss. It is probably more lack of thought than deliberate discrimination, but it needs to be dealt with just as urgently whatever the reason.

Find out also what the people who are sending you expect of you. Often, the conference delegate is made responsible for going through the resolutions beforehand, making recommendations about amendments that can be sent in (see p. 144) and about the way you should be asked to vote. Arc you going to be **mandated**, that is, instructed by your group which way you must vote (see p. 145)? And do you have to report back afterwards? Sorting all this out now will save trouble later.

Putting forward motions

As well as, or instead of, wanting to be a delegate, you may wish to make sure the conference discusses an issue you are particularly concerned about; therefore you want the group to send in a **motion**. Often a branch will send as a delegate the person who proposed the motion they are putting forward. Find out well in advance what the procedure is and whether there are special rules.

■ NUPE says that all motions for its national conference must be national, and not regional or local in character, and must be signed by the chair and secretary of the branch, and stamped with the branch stamp.

You may not have to think up a motion for yourself; one of the groups you support may send you a 'model' one. This may be called other names by different organizations, but it is one that is circulated by a pressure group or outside body to people who are members of that group, and they are asked to put it forward to their branch as the motion to be adopted. The Campaign for Labour Party Democracy, for example, used model motions as the basis of their campaign in the Labour Party for many years. Some organizations, for instance, APEX, forbid these altogether, although they cannot always tell where a motion has come from.

The Labour Party, and some others, say that identical motions only count as one in deciding which are popular enough to have a debate, and so this acts as a discouragement. To get round this, groups will ask you to change a few words in the motion, or add to it or shorten it, so that it is no longer quite the same as any other.

Often there is a rule that issues that were raised last year, or the year before that, cannot be raised again. Motions are usually also restricted to one subject only. **Rule amendments** are usually only allowed at special conferences, perhaps every three years.

These conditions will usually be written down in the rule books or the standing orders. The people in charge of seeing they are carried out are usually called the conference arrangements committee or standing orders committee. In this chapter, they are called the 'organizing committee'. They are a special committee, usually supposed to be independent of any other. They will decide which resolutions are in order and which are not. Within the overall framework of the rules, they will also deal with:

- what order the business should be taken in, and what subjects will be debated;
- how much time is allowed for each subject;
- whether an emergency resolution really is an emergency.

All their decisions are put into a report to the conference, so they can be 'referred back', that is, the organizers can be asked to think again. This point is covered in more detail on pp. 150–51.

These rules are sometimes manipulated by the organizing committee in order to suit themselves or the national executive. They can use them to stop things being discussed that ought to be discussed, for instance, by making a judgement about whether or not something is the 'same subject'. The Labour Party's national conference organizers in particular have done this in the past, and still do to an extent.

Find out the date by which a motion has to be in, and whether there are earlier stages you have to go through. In the Labour Party, for instance, constituency parties have to send in their motions by early July each year. As the motions need to be put forward first of all by **branches** of these parties, they would usually be discussed at their meetings in June. You may also have to notify the branch secretary in advance about a motion, so that it can be circulated with the agenda. (See pp. 37–42 for an explanation of how meetings deal with motions.)

When a motion has been agreed, the secretary should send it off, and in due course it should appear on a list of all the motions for the conference. This is often called the 'preliminary agenda'. This might be a few sheets of paper or, for a bigger conference, a printed book. The fact that it appears here does not necessarily mean that it will be discussed. The decisions on what debates there will be are made later.

A copy may go to the branch secretary, or to you as delegate, or both. Check, as soon as it comes, that the motion your group sent in has been included. If it has been left out by mistake, this can probably be put right; if it has been **ruled out of order**, that is, it has been decided that it does not fit in with the rules laid down for that particular conference, you will have to do some work to try to get it in.

The secretary will have to write **quickly** to the right person at head office to find out why it has been omitted. If the reply comes back that it was ruled out of order, and you think they are wrong and want to fight, you must put together as strong an argument as possible to show that the ruling is wrong. You may also need to arrange for the secretary, or you as the delegate, to go to meet someone in authority, possibly the whole committee, to ask them to change their minds. If this fails, you may have to prepare to ask for a 'reference back' of the organizing committee's report at the beginning of the conference.

Amendments

The next thing is to see if your branch should send in any amendments to other people's motions (amendments are explained on pp. 38–40). Usually there is only a very short time to do this. For the Labour Party, for instance, the book of motions comes out at the end of July and amendments have to be in by mid-August.

Since this is in the middle of the holiday season, it is often difficult to get a meeting together. If you wish to do so, people would need to be forewarned and a date fixed well in advance. If you wait until the preliminary agenda actually appears, you will probably be too late.

Putting in an amendment gives you the chance either to put a point of view on a different subject – perhaps there was another idea for a motion that just got defeated, but people are still interested in it – or to reinforce your original motion by adding something on the same lines to somebody else's motion. If your original motion has been ruled out, it also gives you another chance to get your point across. The same limits to the subjects you can raise will apply to amendments as to motions.

Final agenda

The final list of all the motions and amendments, the final agenda, is sent out between two months and a couple of weeks before the conference. NUPE, for example, say that the final agenda must reach the branch secretary in the first week in April, before their conference in late May.

Some groups, for example, the NCCL, print the agenda in their newsletter, so that everyone can see it. Usually, delegates will also be sent their own copies, but these may not come until later.

Mandating

It is at this stage after the final agenda is issued that delegates are **mandated**, that is, instructed which way to vote. Some groups feel this is too difficult, or that they trust you to behave responsibly, or they are simply lazy about it.

Mandating is important, because it establishes that you are going to the conference not as Ms or Mr Smith, an individual, but as the person representing your group, and accountable to it for your actions. This gives what you are saying and doing greater weight both for the branch and for the conference. Standing up and saying, 'I am the delegate from X branch of 2,000 members, and they have instructed me to say that we must oppose Cruise missiles at all costs', matters a good deal more than saying, 'In my opinion we must oppose Cruise missiles.'

Mandating ought to be encouraged, even though it is tedious and time consuming. So should reporting back afterwards.

People sometimes object to mandating, on the grounds that it leaves people with no independent mind of their own, but this really is not true. The mandating meeting will not know what issues will turn out to be particularly important when you get there, or how different motions will be composited together (see p. 148).

There is always a need for the delegate to exercise his or her judgement and interpret what the group means. What it does is to make sure that the delegate knows what the group's general line is and, if it is combined with insisting on reporting back, it is a reasonable safeguard to ensure that s/he sticks to it. You can never be certain of preventing someone doing the opposite of what they were told to do, of course, but you should at least find out about it this way, and be able to ensure that they do not become delegate in the future.

The simplest way to mandate is to concentrate on the half dozen major issues that will be coming up – perhaps using a press report that will have picked out the biggest questions – and take an attitude on that. So in 1984, you might have needed to decide whether you want your union or party to affiliate to CND or not, or what attitude to take on government anti-union legislation.

A more thorough method, but one that can take up a lot of time, is to go through all the motions in the book and decide on an attitude. Unless everyone has had a chance to see all the motions, someone has to summarize them and also to remind the meeting about what policy you have already decided on, perhaps in a motion about the subject a few months ago. Here is an example of part of what one Labour Party produced for its mandating meeting:

> *Notes on Conference Agenda*
> The delegate will be expected to support composite motions which reflect current Anytown Labour Party policy. The party does not have a policy on items marked *, so needs to take a decision on whether they are for or against these proposals.
> Motions 61–77 Women's Organizations:
> * Mandatory women on every parliamentary shortlist (68)
> * Target of filling half the places on NEC subcommittee with women (69)
>
> 78–81 Positive Discrimination:
> * Working party to be set up for greater involvement at all levels of party of disadvantaged groups (79)
>
> 108–113 Witch Hunts:
> Anytown policy to oppose any witch hunts.
> * calls for reinstatement of *Militant* editorial board (108)
> * removes power of NEC to expel (114)
> * restricts power to conference (109)

Usually a group would require a special meeting to fit everything in. It then goes through the list of motions section by section. Where no one is interested in an issue, it would just be passed over or left to the discretion of the delegate. Existing policy would not usually be changed at this type of meeting. Where it needed clarifying, or there was none, there might be a short debate so that there is some guidance for the delegate. If there is to be an election, for instance, for the leadership and the national executive of the Labour Party, there might also be a ballot (see p. 47) to decide who you should vote for.

How to put the mandate into practice, once you get there, is discussed on p. 156.

Essential documents

You'll probably only get the final papers, and detailed instructions, in the last few weeks or days before the conference. Read through them carefully, not only to check when and where you are supposed to be, but also to make sure you have been sent all the right papers. There may be a general secretary's or executive council report, and perhaps some supplementary reports. There should be a delegate's **credential** – a card or badge – and, if you are the only delegate or the leader of a delegation, also a voting card or a book of voting papers (see p. 156 for an explanation of the different methods of voting). Some organizations, such as the TUC, also provide a separate 'wallet card' which you hand over in return for a wallet full of last-minute papers once you arrive. Sometimes you have to show your delegate's card or have a slip torn off it. You may also have a plan showing the location of your seat. If anything appears to be missing, phone up in advance to find out what has happened. If there's been a mistake, they can probably set aside a copy for you to pick up specially.

People who are not delegates but **visitors** may receive only the agenda paper and a badge. They are unlikely to receive all the reports, or the programme of business. They may be able to pick them up at the conference, or possibly to buy copies from the bookstall.

The first morning of a conference usually begins later than other days, because people have to show their delegate's credentials, collect the various papers, and perhaps also be ticked off on a list or sign for things. The most important papers are:

- the list of **composites**;
- the report of the organizing committee and the programme of business;
- the ballot paper if there are to be any elections.

If this is the first time you have been to conference, try to arrange beforehand to meet someone – perhaps the leader of your delegation, or a friend – on the first day, so that they can explain to you what is going to happen and where everything is. A conference can be extremely confusing the first time, even if you've briefed yourself in advance.

Timetable

This will be set out in the papers you collect on the first day, usually as part of the organizing committee's report.

Here is an example of part of one, taken from the regional conference of the Labour Party in London:

Timetable for Regional Conference
Saturday 5 March

10 a.m.	Appointment of Scrutineers and Tellers Standing Orders Committee Report
10.20	Address by the Chair
10.30	Executive Report
10.40	CAMPAIGNING; Composite L FINANCES; Affiliation fees and donations
11.00	Proposed Amendments to Rules and Standing Orders Motions 5, 7, 8, 14

11.30 GLC Report
12.00 Fraternal Delegates' Address

The programme lists what time each debate is going to happen, and also which motions are being debated. It is only now that you will discover what subjects are going to be discussed and what motions on the subjects are going to be taken.

Organizations have different methods of deciding what subjects are to be discussed. In some groups, including major unions, they work through everything, but motions on the same subject are grouped together in one debate. In APEX, almost all the discussion is on the Executive Report, and very few motions arc ever debated, while in the Labour Party, the organizing committee chooses the subjects, on the basis of how many motions have come in on each subject, how controversial the issue is, and whether there is a chance of embarrassment for the executive (which they try to avoid). The National Union of Students hold a postal ballot in advance among their organizations on the subjects to be discussed. The Tory Party's organizers select the main subjects, but leave time for a small number of motions, selected by the delegates through a vote.

What motions are going to be discussed in each debate? Some organizations aim to discuss every motion on the subjects they have picked. Others select a few. The practice by which they select varies between organizations; it may be laid down in the standing orders, alternatively you may have to ask someone who has been at the conference before. Have they selected the right ones?

If they have got things wrong, from your point of view, possible ways of dealing with it are to go to see the organizing committee about it, or to move reference back of their report (see p. 151).

In either case, you will get further if there is a group backing a particular viewpoint, rather than a single individual, so look for other delegates whose motions have been similarly squeezed out. Link up with them and take any action as a united group.

Compositing

Before some but not all big conferences, a lot of work will go into fitting motions on the same subject together, getting some amendments accepted and others withdrawn, so that everything can be fitted into the timetable. This is called **compositing**.

Several motions are put together as one, and are then referred to as **composite motions** or simply **composites**. The rules about how to do this vary between different organizations. The Labour Party has very strict rules, where you are allowed only to use words which appear in one of the motions you're putting together. You can leave some of them out, but you must not put anything in.

For instance, on p. 40 there was an example of a motion by Peter Pickard. 'This meeting supports the strikers and all members agree to donate £5 a week to their hardship fund.' Suppose there was another, from Alan Wilkinson, saying, 'This meeting considers that the methods the government are using in policing the strikers' pickets are totally undemocratic. We pledge our support to the strikers.'

These two motions could be composited together in several ways. The easiest would be to add the first sentence of Alan's motion to the end of Peter's. The second sentence of Alan's then drops out altogether, since it doesn't say anything that isn't in Peter's motion.

Most organizations are less strict than the Labour Party and allow the odd new word to make the composite read better.

Composites are often much more complicated than this example; they may include up to a dozen motions and amendments, and cover a page and a half. It is not easy to pick one's way through them or to be sure that they make sense.

For a big conference, compositing is sometimes done by post, or there may be a separate meeting several weeks before the conference, or the day or the morning before. The delegate from the branch or group sending the motion is responsible for looking after it during this process.

If a delegate doesn't respond to a letter about compositing, or doesn't turn up to a meeting about it, the rules usually say that the motion s/he was responsible for **falls**, which means it is dropped and not discussed at all.

Try to check beforehand what the rules and practices are in your particular organization. Ask someone who's been before, or phone up the conference organizers and discuss it with them. Don't leave it until you get to the conference, because by then everyone likely to understand the process will be very busy, either organizing or plotting, and you may have missed the procedural boat.

In some organizations, the TUC for instance, the paid officials write draft composites. If you want to get your own way, write your own draft. Try to get in as many bits from other people's motions as you can, so that they will support you. You will have to do some negotiating to get a final draft acceptable to everyone and then do a deal on who is **proposing** and who is **seconding**; these are the people who have the chance to make the longest speeches. For example, you might have to abandon your wish to propose, and allow someone who has agreed to let part of his/her motion disappear into the composite propose the motion instead.

The most important points are:

- to get in any special points that appear in your motion and in no one else's. For instance, in a series of fairly similar motions about the NHS, yours might be the only one that mentions women's health, so that is the part you would want to get in.
- to avoid your motion being put together with others with which you don't agree, or that are more extreme than yours and so are likely to be defeated. For example, your motion might call for the renationalization of parts of British Steel, with the price originally being paid for them being given in compensation. Another motion might say they should be renationalized 'without compensation'. Your branch may have decided during the mandating process (see p. 145) whether they would have supported a motion written in those terms, or you may be able to guess from their attitudes in other discussions. If not, they are unlikely to be very happy about your backing it now.

Once motions have been composited, the original ones are treated as **withdrawn** in favour of the composite (see p. 42). The person or group putting forward the motion has to grant permission before it is composited. Having turned up at the meeting, you can therefore sit tight and refuse to co-operate if you want your group's view to stand by itself. However, you may find that motions not composited are not given time to be discussed properly, are separated from the main debate, or even left out altogether, so think carefully about what is best. It's sensible to get the support of your organization beforehand, when you are being mandated, if you think you may have to refuse to join in a composite because your motion will not fit happily with any of the others.

Once all the composites have been put together, they are printed up, or duplicated, and handed out to all the delegates. There are cases, for instance, at the national Labour Party conference, where the process of putting composites together goes on throughout the week, and the new ones may turn up at the beginning of any session. This will be partly the result of the organizers putting pressure on people who have so far refused to composite, telling them that if they refuse to comply they will not have their motion debated at all. Those people will be feeling increasingly harassed as time seeps away, and therefore more willing to concede.

Organizing committee's report

The committee responsible for organizing and running the

conference will usually work within the framework of the organization's rules or standing orders, but often has the power to vary them if it considers this necessary. At a big conference, they will usually provide a written report and add a spoken announcement at the beginning of the conference, and at the start of other sessions also if necessary.

The written report of the conference arrangements, or standing orders, may cover, for instance, such things as:

- the length of time they are allocating for each speaker;
- when the elections are going to take place;
- the position when a resolution is not reached; is it remitted (see p. 156) to the executive or is it dropped altogether?

What it gives you are details of the mechanics of the conference. To know what is really going to happen, listen carefully to the **spoken** report that the chair of the organizing committee will give at the very beginning of the conference, and possibly at the beginning of several other sessions. In the report, s/he will start by formally moving acceptance of the written report, and then go on to state:

- what emergency motions have been received, and which ones have been accepted and which ruled out (see p. 39 for an explanation of this);
- when they are going to be debated, if at all;
- any alterations to the written programme of business, including perhaps the times when 'fraternal delegates', who are representatives from sympathetic organizations, will speak;
- any other points on which there has been, or may be, a problem.

At some conferences, as soon as the chair of the organizing committee sits down, one finds a stream of people 'moving reference back' of the report; in other words, complaining that it is not satisfactory.

An alert member might have picked up the fact that they have not left time for a debate on, say, nuclear disarmament. So s/he goes up to the rostrum at the end of the report and says, 'I move reference back because this very important issue is not being discussed,' and explains why. If this is seconded, the chair then takes a vote on whether the conference supports the reference back. Delegates are often very confused about what they are voting for, and may think they are supporting the organizing committee by voting for the reference back. However, those who would count as the 'establishment' – at the Labour Party, the big trade-union blocs – almost always support the organizers. If a reference back is carried, then the organizing committee has to think again. They should then find a place on the agenda for the debate.

Occasionally they sit tight and refuse to change their decision. Their ultimate weapon is to threaten to resign as a committee, which would then leave the conference with no one to organize it, which would create a crisis. Usually some sort of compromise is worked out well before this, but while the negotiations are going on, it is a matter of whose nerve cracks first, the organizers' or the delegates' pressing their point of view.

Sometimes attempts to refer back are organized in advance, perhaps when a whole group of motions on one subject has been ruled out of order, and so a string of people get up and complain about the same thing. More usually, however, people have to react spontaneously because they have little time to find out what's happening or to discuss it with other people; this is one of the ways in which the organizers maintain their dominance: they know what is happening better than anyone else. At some conferences, for instance, the Labour Party, it's important to make your protest even if it seems as if no notice will be taken of it, because otherwise it gives the organizers the chance to say, 'Well, no one complained at the time.' Often the organizers will ask the person to come to see them in order to try to resolve the problem. If they don't, a determined person can raise the issue each time they report, even after the time for that subject has passed on the timetable, and be a nuisance until something is sorted out.

On **emergency** motions, the position is slightly different. Here the organizers can always be overruled by the conference. The organizers will **recommend** that motion X is, or is not, an emergency, but the conference then votes on this, and if they vote that motion X **is** an emergency, that is final. It has been known at the Labour Party conference for the organizers to fail to find time to debate a motion that has been agreed as an emergency against their wishes; but that is unusual.

There are conferences where references back are very rare. Find out the position at your particular conference by asking someone who's been there before.

Once all the references back have been dealt with, the report is voted on formally.

Tellers and scrutineers

Tellers and scrutineers are the people who count the votes and are appointed before the conference debates start. The **tellers** count hands, or cards, or take ballot boxes around to the delegates; the **scrutineers** sit in a back room counting ballot papers, once a vote has closed.

For a big conference, they are usually selected by the organizers beforehand, and you are asked to agree a whole list of names at the beginning. This is called agreement *en bloc*. It is a responsible but boring job, and it can mean that people are out of the room for long periods while they are counting votes; therefore not many people want to take it on.

There is usually a group of people who have been doing the job for years and who are considered reliable by the organizers. If you don't trust the tellers, you could get your branch to nominate you, but it will be difficult to shift them, especially since a conference will not be very interested in the question and will not care whom it votes for; unless, that is, there have been allegations of fiddling, in which case it could become a lively issue.

Going in and out of the hall

You do not have to stay in the hall all the time; but make sure you are there at the time when your motion is due to come up, because it would 'fall' (that is, not be discussed) in your absence.

Each time you re-enter the hall, you will probably have to show your credential, that is, your badge or card, to the stewards who are sitting at each door of the hall. The people doing this job might be the staff of the organization, or volunteers from the local branch, Labour Party or trades council. They are ordinary people, often not too confident of what they are doing, so they may become officious and difficult. Usually it's best simply to appreciate their problems, if you can, and bite back your annoyance. Occasionally you will encounter a steward who is very sexist or racist, so that you feel you have to complain publicly. You could do this by raising a point of order (see p. 43), reporting exactly what's happened, and asking the chair to ensure that it stops.

The debates

Conference debates are run differently from those of an ordinary branch or committee meeting. They need to be more formal, because of the larger numbers involved, and they are usually also dealing with a whole series of motions, rather than just one or two. They may also include discussion of the **report** given by the executive or general council, and of any policy documents they are putting forward, though the procedure here varies between groups. To understand how it works, take the example of a debate on health.

■ There is one composite on community care, and another on privatization, and two motions standing on their own about maternity provision and mental handicap. There is also a section of the executive council report on these matters. This is proposed by the executive council member, who briefly says what they have been up to in the last year. Then the motions are proposed. The composites have precedence, that is, they are proposed first.
So Bill proposes Composite A, and Mary seconds him, and then Leroy proposes Composite B, and Shakil seconds him. At this point the ordinary motions are proposed and seconded and the debate is 'thrown open'. This is the stage at which ordinary delegates have the chance to speak. You are then entitled to talk about **any** of the motions that have been proposed and seconded, or about several of them or about the executive report. So Lorraine might want to make a point about maternity care, and then Kevin might spell out his branch's attitude to each motion.

Often, however, there is a lot of competition to speak, and not much room for the ordinary lay delegate. The speakers from the floor could be people who agreed to withdraw, or composite, a motion on condition that they got the chance to speak, or well-known faces, or people with special knowledge about the subject, or simply the chair's favourites. Even if it is blatantly obvious that the latter is the case, the chair will usually deny it and claim that s/he is being fair. None the less it is worth complaining, because s/he may tone down his/her behaviour.

There are usually strict time limits on speeches.

■ At the London Labour Party Conference, the limits were:
movers of composite motions 7 minutes;
seconders 4 minutes;
movers of other motions 5 minutes;
seconders 3 minutes;
movers of reports 10 minutes;
all other speakers 3 minutes.

The leader of your organization and any important visiting speaker, however, is usually allowed to exceed these limits.

At most conferences of any size, one has to speak from a rostrum. This reading desk on a small raised platform often has a set of lights: either red, yellow and green, or just red and green. The chair, or possibly someone sitting beside him/her to help out, will time each speech and switch the light to yellow when there is a minute or so to go, and then red when time has run out. If there is no yellow, they may flash the red light when there is a minute to go. The chair may interrupt people who go over the time limit and tell them to finish; s/he may even turn off the microphone if they go on. People do go over time, of course, especially important people (or those that think they are), but conferences get rather impatient with them, and it doesn't do their case any good.

It is usually laid down that a speaker must give his/her name, and say where s/he represents, at the beginning of his/her speech. Anyone who does not do so is liable to have people shouting, 'Name,' until they comply. This rule is there because if the conference is being recorded or taken down in shorthand, it will help the people carrying out the task. It also means that people who don't know everyone can find out who's speaking, and what special knowledge they have. If, for example, the NUPE members in Walsall have had a long and bitter strike against privatization, then if a member from that branch speaks about campaigning on this s/he will be assumed to have much more knowledge than someone from a branch that's done nothing.

This book is not the place for a guide to public speaking, but a few points may be helpful. The conference will probably be the biggest place you've ever spoken in, as well as to the largest number of people. But this doesn't matter, because you'll have a microphone to help, so talk in the sort of voice you would use at a branch meeting, clear and confident, but not a shout. Women have to take special care to pitch their voices low, otherwise they can start squeaking. Don't stand too close to the microphone, because doing so makes it whistle. Give your name and branch, and tell people what motion you're supporting or opposing right at the start. If it's your first speech, you may want to write everything down first, but try not to read it out word for word, as that sounds stilted. One possibility is to write down a series of headings on small cards, for the main points, and use them to jog your memory. Unless you're very confident, it's best not to try jokes or flights of rhetoric the first time. If they don't come off, you'll feel very deflated. Finally, however nervous you are, plough on regardless. Once you've got that first speech over, no future one can ever be so nerve-racking.

At any point during the debate, a delegate can raise a 'point of order'. The various points were explained in Chapter 2; any of them could be raised, unless your standing orders specifically rule them out. If a group is trying to change the way the conference works, or disrupt it, there may be a great many 'points of order'.

At the end of the debate, a member of the governing body of your organization replies or 'sums up'. They may try to summarize the debate, or they may express their own views. Executives usually ask a different person to reply to each debate, so that often it will be clear that the person replying does not know much about the subject.

This person is supposed to tell you what the recommendation of the executive is, regarding whether you should support or oppose the motion. If there are a lot of motions, they will have to tell you about each one. They will usually say why, when they are recommending you to turn a motion down, and often what they say is, 'We'd love to support this motion, except for the little section which goes way beyond our policy, so we can't do it.' Alternatively they may say they support the motion **with reservations**. This means they are not going to feel bound by the part they don't like, so it is only half a loaf, although better than being defeated.

They could also ask that you **withdraw** or **remit** your motion. Withdrawing it means that it is dropped altogether, while remitting means that the executive promises to have a look at it. Either way there will be no vote.

At the TUC and Labour Party conferences, a lot of pressure is put on people with uncomfortable or controversial motions to 'remit' without a vote. At the Labour Party conference, for example, the person replying to a motion on behalf of the national executive committee may say, 'We'd like to support motion XX but there's one sentence which causes us difficulty because we don't think it's practical, so we are asking you to remit, and we will look at it more closely.' If the mover accepts, the chair ought to ask the delegates to vote on whether they want the motion to be remitted. This is because the motion is now the 'property of the meeting' (see p. 42) and it's not for the delegate to take a decision on it by himself/herself. However, since remission is used by executive committees as a way of ducking an issue (sometimes quite sensibly), this often isn't done. It's also customary that if the mover, or the meeting, refused to remit, the executive will recommend the meeting to vote against the motion.

Voting

At the end of each debate, the conference votes on the motions. In most cases, they will be passed if there is a simple majority (that is, half those voting plus one) in favour. For some things, for instance changing the rules or rescinding a previous motion, you may need a two-thirds majority. This will be spelt out in the standing orders or the rule book. In the case of the Labour Party, a motion has to be passed by a two-thirds majority to be sure of a place in the manifesto, although a simple majority is enough to make it party policy.

Usually the chair will ask for a 'show of hands' on each motion. That is, you simply raise your arms and s/he judges how many there are on each side rather than actually counting. Don't be surprised if a good many of the motions go through very quickly, with large majorities in support. At any conference there will be a large number of motions which are simply re-affirming previous policy, and since everyone basically agrees, the vote is only a formality.

In some cases, for instance the TUC, the organizers try very hard to keep controversial issues off the agenda, because they want to maintain a show of unity. Generally there will be only two or three big set-piece debates at a conference, on the issues that are really dividing the movement that year, and there will be broad agreement on most other things.

If, however, it is an important matter, or if it looks as if the numbers are fairly even, the chair may decide to have a **card vote**. Alternatively, delegates themselves may call for one – literally, they will stand up and shout, 'Card vote.' They must do this either before the show of hands or **immediately** after it. In the Labour Party, the constitution says that if anyone calls for a card vote, the chair must take one, but in practice if only a few people are calling for one s/he often ignores them. In other organizations, if a specific number of people are standing and calling for a card vote, the rules say that the chair has to take it. NUPE, for instance, says that there must be at least 30 people requesting such a vote.

A **card vote** means that the number of members that each delegate represents is counted, rather than the delegates themselves. There are two main methods of running a card vote. One is used by the Labour Party, the other by the TUC. Other organizations use one or the other, depending on the custom which has grown up.

In the Labour Party, you are given a book of voting papers, marked with the number of votes you have (rather than putting 1,000 or 1,000,000 they put 1, or 1,000). The papers to use for each vote are numbered, so perhaps you will have Card Vote No. 1 during the debate on the first day, and then Nos. 2 and 3 on the next, and so on through the week. For each vote, you have **two** papers, one for and one against. When a card vote is happening, the tellers come round with a ballot box, and you put in one voting paper, for or against, and tear up the other one, or put it somewhere else. The tellers then take the boxes away, the scrutineers count up, and the result of the vote is announced later.

This system can make it fairly easy for the leader of a delegation to disobey the wishes of the rest, or even the mandate that s/he was given by his/her own union's conference or executive, because people may not be able to see what voting paper actually goes into the box. There's a long history of trouble over this, and as a result the Labour Party has now begun recording which way people vote, on certain issues.

The TUC method makes it more difficult to go against the wishes of a delegation, though not impossible. Here, the person responsible for casting the vote has just one card, with the number of votes printed on it, again one vote per thousand. The chair then asks everyone voting in favour to stand and show their cards; the tellers write down the numbers and give the paper to the chief teller. Then the same happens for the no votes, the totals are added up there and then and the result announced.

Delegation votes

A delegation of more than one or two people will usually have a leader who actually casts the vote. S/he will be the most senior person on the delegation, so at a union conference the leader might be the branch chair and at the TUC it would be a member of the national executive or the general secretary of your union. The methods used to decide which way to vote vary. The GMBATU, for example, entrusts the decision at Labour Party and TUC conferences to the members of their executive council, who all attend the conference as delegates, and the extra lay delegates who are elected from the regions are simply told which way to vote.

In other instances, however, a meeting is held just before the beginning of the conference, once they know what motions and composites are coming forward, and the delegates systematically go through the list deciding on which way to vote, even before they have heard the debate.

In most cases, once the decision has been taken, all the votes of that group go in the same direction. So the AUEW, for instance, casts all its 1,000 votes for or against a motion, even if the delegation voted very narrowly on that course of action. This is called the 'block voting system'. It is very rare for union rules to allow for a delegation's votes to be split, although it does happen occasionally.

Something important, however, might come up during the conference itself, like an emergency resolution or new information about a particular subject. Then the delegation may have extra meetings first thing in the morning, or during the lunch hour, or even during the conference itself. Sometimes you see a whole delegation leaving a conference at once, while a debate is taking place – this is so that they can decide what to do. Sometimes, however, the delegates don't wish to leave the hall, or there is no time. Then another method is used for the leader to pass a notepad round the delegation, asking people to write down 'Yes' or 'No'; then add them up and vote accordingly. In any case, the delegation should be voting in line with the policy of the union, or of the branch, and the only question should be one of interpretation.

Elections

At most conferences there are elections, perhaps of the national executive, perhaps of the union president, or other officers. In some cases these will be formalities; there may be only one candidate, or only one that people take seriously. With these, the election might be by a 'show of hands' (see p. 157), but where there is a real contest, you will have a **ballot**.

This usually takes place near the beginning of the conference, so that there is time for the results to be counted and announced before the delegates leave. There will be a closing time for the ballot, which will be announced by the chair or written down in the programme of business, or both. The ballot boxes are usually by the desks of the people running the conference, where the papers are handed out on the first day. You should be told where they are. If you cannot find them, ask a steward.

One person, usually the leader of the delegation, must collect the ballot papers, fill them in and take them to the ballot box.

Who to vote for should have been decided in the delegate meeting that agreed your attitude to the motions (see p. 158).

Voting arrangements can be quite complicated. For some jobs, everyone in the conference may be entitled to vote; for others, it may only be certain groups. For example, at the TUC, everyone can vote for the general secretary (though they don't often get the chance, since 1984 was the first year that the election was ever contested). Everyone can also vote for the women's seats on the general council. However, while the large unions automatically have other seats, the smaller unions have to vote among themselves for their representatives.

In other cases the voting may be done by district. In the Greater London Labour Party, for instance, London is divided into four districts, each of which has four people on the executive, and the constituency Labour Parties for that area vote for their representatives, while the unions have their own group.

There are several voting systems that can be used, but the two main ones are **first past the post** and **alternative voting**. These are described on p. 131, together with a third system, **exhaustive ballot**, which is not often used at conferences because it is difficult to put into practice.

The votes are then counted by the **scrutineers** (see p. 47) and the result is announced to the conference. Many sets of conference papers include the list of nominees, so you can mark on it who got elected and who did not. They may also print or duplicate 'results sheets' for you to collect before the end, providing the details. It is worth taking these because they save you trouble when you are reporting back as you can pass the list round the meeting instead of having to read a list of names out.

Outside the conference

At a major conference, there is often as much going on outside the conference hall as there is inside. Often there are 'fringe' meetings, at lunchtime or in the evenings, of various national groups or factions in your organization. Often a conference diary is issued listing all the various events. If there is not one with your papers, ask at the enquiries or press desk. There may also be meetings that did not get into the diary because they were not organized in time or involve unofficial groups, so look out for posters and leaflets.

Reporting back

Some groups send people to all sorts of conferences and never ask them what went on. Even if your organization has not asked people to report in the past, it is useful to suggest that you should do so, and set a precedent for other people, especially if you think the group's views are not being properly represented in some places.

You can report in writing, or verbally, or both. Probably the best way is to write a report and circulate it either before or at the meeting, and then answer any other questions people may have. If you have been sent by several branches, try to attend meetings of all of them to give your report.

People will want to know:

- how you voted; did you follow their mandate (see p. 145) or, in any case where that was difficult, what did you do?
- whether you spoke, and especially whether you talked about questions of particular concern to the group.
- what other speakers said that was particularly important to your group. A health service branch of GMBATU, for instance, would want to know much more about the health

service debate at the union conference than about the discussion of shipbuilding.

- what happened to the branch's resolution or amendment. If it was composited (see p. 148) with others, make copies of the composite or put details in your report. Tell them whether it was carried or lost and what the national executive speaker said about it.

What people **don't** need is a blow-by-blow account of how each day went, which will be fairly boring and take up a great deal of time. Hang on to the programme of business, and the agenda, and pass it round the meeting so that anyone who is interested can have a look. It's worth giving your general impression of the atmosphere of the conference, but not at great length. If leaflets were handed out, you could pass these round, together with any press cuttings you may have picked up. If people have the chance to ask questions, they can always raise any points that you haven't mentioned but which may be of interest to them.

Finally, once the conference is over, the resolutions it passed are meant to be translated into action rather than simply forgotten. If your branch had an important resolution, you will want to follow up what happened to it. Does your national executive publish its minutes? Keep an eye on any discussions in those, or for any reports in the journal. If after, say, six months you have not seen anything there, or have not received any correspondence about the resolution, the branch could write and enquire about progress. This would be especially necessary if you have remitted the motion (see p. 156) to the executive for them to deal with, perhaps under pressure and with a promise that they will take the question up urgently.

Checklist

This list assumes you are planning to go to a conference for the first time as a delegate, taking with you a motion suggested by you and voted through by your group. Look at it when you first make your plans, and again before you get to the conference. For those who are more experienced, it may also be a useful way of jogging your memory.

Check well in advance — clause in your rules

(a) When motions have to be in; (pp. 142–4) ______
what form they must take; (pp. 142–4) ______
what subjects are allowed; (pp. 142–4) ______
the meeting of your group at which they will be discussed. (pp. 142–4) ______

(b) When the delegate(s) are elected; (pp. 139–42) ______
any special qualifications they need; (pp. 139–42) ______
what the procedure is for electing them; (pp. 139–42) ______
who has been the delegate for previous years, and whether s/he wants to go again. (pp. 139–42) ______

(c) What the timetable is for the
preliminary agenda (p. 143) ______
amendments (p. 144) ______
the final agenda (p. 144) ______

Check closer to the conference date

(a) as **delegate**
the date and time you have to be at the conference; (p. 141) ______
the arrangements for
accommodation (p. 141) ______
expenses (p. 141) ______
crèche (p. 141) ______
any other special needs. (p. 142) ______

(b) on **procedure**
are motions composited together? If so,
When and how does this take place? (p. 148) ______
How do they select subjects and motions for debate? (p. 148) ______
Are you going to be allowed to speak on it, or will it only be the leader of your delegation? (p. 154) ______
How do the delegation make up their minds about which way to vote? (p. 158) ______

(c) on the **agenda**

When the preliminary agenda is published, is your motion in it? (p. 144) ______

If not, why not? (p. 144) ______

What can you do about it? (p. 144) ______

Are there amendments you want to put in? (p. 144) ______

What is the procedure, and the deadline, for them? (p. 144) ______

What other motions are there on your subject? (p. 144) ______

When the final agenda is published

is your motion/amendment in? (p. 144) ______

if not, why not? (p. 144) ______

What can you do about it? (p. 144) ______

what other important changes are there? (p. 144) ______

(d) on **mandating**

When are you being mandated? (p. 145) ______

What procedure is going to be used? (p. 145) ______

What is left to your discretion? (p. 145) ______

Have you made a detailed note of the instructions? (p. 146) ______

At the conference itself

Have you:

got your credentials? (p. 147) ______

picked up the extra papers? (p. 147) ______

picked up your voting card and ballot papers? (p. 147) ______

found someone who knows what's going on and will explain to you? (p. 148) ______

What's the conference timetable? (p. 148) ______

When is your motion/amendment coming up? (p. 148) ______

If you want to speak, how long have you got? (p. 154) ______

Have you worked out what you are going to say? (p. 154) ______

On the organizing committee's report

Do you want to ask for anything to be referred back? (p. 150) ______

Or to support someone else's reference back? (p. 150) ______

Do you have to go to see the committee about anything? (p. 150) ______

During the debates

Are you keeping a note (for your report) on important issues? (p. 100) ______

how you voted? (p. 100) ______

whether you spoke and what you said? (p. 100) ______

other speakers who are important for your group? (p. 100) ________
what happened? (p. 100) ________

Afterwards

Have you assembled all the papers? (p. 161) ________
written your report? (p. 161) ________
circulated it? (p. 161) ________
followed up any useful contacts? (p. 161) ________
claimed your expenses? (p. 161) ________

8.

Running your own conference

This chapter is intended to help people with enthusiasm, but limited experience and resources who have to run a conference, rather than attending as a delegate. It will also be relevant to anyone taking part for the first time in the decision-making process of an established conference, for example, if you become a member of a trade union's conference arrangements committee (see p. 150).

Preparations

As with ordinary meetings, the first step is to look at the minimum that is necessary. The aim of a big decision-making conference is to create, or to change, policy for the organization. So people need:

- to have the chance to put forward proposals for decision;
- to know in good time what decisions are to be taken;
- to discuss the questions and reach a considered view;
- to know afterwards what the results are.

The organizing committee, therefore, needs to start, probably soon after the last conference, by drawing up a timetable for the run-up to the conference. If you work backwards from the conference date itself, allowing sufficient time for each task, this will give you an idea of how far in advance you need to start.

■ Ellen's playscheme federation decides on a conference in mid-June. Since most of their groups meet once a month, they will all need to have the final papers, with all the items to be discussed, at least a month ahead in mid-May. To get the papers ready will take a fortnight, so proposals and papers for discussion will need to be with the committee at the beginning of May.

Having got this far back, however, you cannot go any further without knowing more about how you are going to organize the conference itself. Are you going to have motions, amendments to motions, several motions which are similar, put together into one or two longer ones?

If you are having motions, local groups need time to discuss them and need to know when they must be sent in by and to whom. If groups are allowed to suggest changes (amendments) to the motions sent in by other groups, then they must first of all know what they are; so copies of the motions must be sent round in time for them to be discussed, and usually you should allow at least a month for this.

If, having received copies of the motions from the groups, you wish to amalgamate the ones that are similar, how are you going to arrange this?

The formal procedure is called 'compositing' (see p. 148). If you want to ask groups to agree on how their motions can be put together, in advance of the conference, you will also need to allow time for them to get in touch and exchange letters and phone calls – a fortnight at least.

So returning to the example of Ellen's group, they have to deal with motions, amendments and composites. They must therefore allow a month for the motions to be sent in; then another month for people to send in amendments; and a fortnight for the motions and amendments to be put together.

They also need time to do the mailings; they think they can do this in a week, but as they are a small voluntary group this involves them working quite hard; a group that could not pull out all the stops would have to allow longer. So this means that they need three months altogether for the process, before the agenda has to be prepared. So the latest they can send out their initial mailing is 1 February.

If, having planned all this, you realize you have taken on more than your group can handle, now is the time to decide what to cut out, not later when you have made promises and raised people's expectations.

At this early stage you should decide on a rough timetable (see p. 170) for each day and send invitations to any speakers or special guests you want to come.

Motions

A motion, which in a few sentences spells out a precise view on something, has the advantage of giving people something specific to focus on. An alternative is to have rather longer 'papers', spelling out the arguments as well as a final conclusion. But these are more difficult for people to digest and it can be awkward to know how to go about changing them. People will get confused if there is a set of amendments, perhaps involving a dozen different changes to various paragraphs throughout a long document. It is even worse if you have more than one set of amendments on this basis.

The argument that is put in favour of a long paper is that it is otherwise very difficult for delegates to grasp the arguments and therefore have an informed discussion. This, however, can be dealt with by asking people to provide **background** papers for any motion, making it clear that these are there simply for information about what the arguments are. Only the motion itself can be amended. However, think before you arrange for this about duplicating or copying facilities. Have you the resources to deal with large amounts of paper, and can your group afford the costs of paper and postage? Will your members read all this literature anyway?

If the planning group cannot cope with sending out a lot of extra papers, here are alternatives:

- Tell people that they must supply the right number of copies of any paper they want sent out, and possibly also that they must pay the cost of any extra postage.
- Supply anyone who wants to send out a paper with a copy of the mailing list, and let them get on with it.

Both of these solutions, though, simply pass the problem down the line to the groups themselves; there may be no satisfactory answer. One other possibility is for the planning group, or another smaller group, itself to write a policy paper and ask people to amend that. Again, you might want them only to amend the conclusions, rather than the arguments, to keep things simple. Other groups may want to prepare alternative papers; try to insist that they contain clear summaries and a list of conclusions that other people can focus on.

First mailing

This should say:

- when the conference will be;
- where it is, and what the arrangements are. Is it residential? Is there a crèche? How long will it go on for each day? The nuts and bolts of running a conference are covered in Chapter 12 of *Organising Things* (see Further Reading, p. 210);
- how people are to be appointed, or selected, to attend;
- what the timetable in the run-up to the conference is. Give people definite deadlines, and make it clear that you will stick to them.

Tell people also what the guidelines for motions are. For instance, are you restricted to covering only local, or only national, subjects? Can you cover only things that are **directly** related to the group's aims, or range wider than that? Are there subjects which you are not allowed to discuss? All these questions should be covered in the standing orders or the constitution, or there may be a custom which has grown up over the years which is accepted by the members.

For example, Jack's group has a clause in its constitution saying that it is 'non-party political'. This would mean that it could not discuss affiliation to the Labour Party, unless first of all there was a rule change altering this clause.

Other questions of this sort include:

- whether changes in the rules can be discussed at any conference, or only special ones;
- whether subjects that were discussed last year can be covered again this year?

If you explain all these points on a single sheet of paper, to go out in the first mailing, it will reduce the number of wasted motions which you have to rule out of order (see p. 144). It may also help to clarify things in your own minds as organizers, if you work out these points early on.

Who are you mailing out to? Depending on your constitution, it might be the secretary of each group or individual members. If it is the secretaries of groups, then you also need a way of alerting individual members to the fact that the conference is taking place, in case they cannot get to a local meeting, or the secretary is inefficient and forgets to mention it. If you have a national magazine or newsletter, put a summary of the main points in your first circular into that. The important issues will be the date of the conference, the key dates in the pre-conference timetable, and how people are appointed to attend.

The work of dealing with the responses could be divided among the planning group. It will be easiest if each person takes one task; one to register the delegates, for instance, and another to acknowledge the motions as they are sent in. Either a sub-group, or the whole of the planning group, should look at each motion and decide whether it fits with the guidelines. This probably means having a special meeting as soon as the deadline for all motions has passed.

Where a motion does not fit, you then need to:

- tell the group concerned, with an explanation of why you are ruling it out of order;

- tell them how they can challenge the decisions. This will often be laid down in your constitution. In many cases, it means asking the whole conference to decide; the group needs to know how to go about this.

Second mailing

Having decided which motions are **in order** and which are not, you then need to send them **all** out so that people can see what they can amend. Many organizations do not circulate the motions that have been ruled out of order; however, it is better if you do, together with a note of the reasons. If the motions simply disappear, this gives the organizers considerable power, so if you are committed to keeping people informed, you should tell them what is **not** being discussed, as well as what is.

If you have a newsletter or magazine, you could include all the motions in this. NCCL, for instance, does this, and it means that all the members, not just the local group secretaries, can see what they are.

In your mailing, and in any report in the magazine, reprint the timetable and the procedure for amendments. Don't assume that people will necessarily remember from the previous mailing. When the amendments come in, they too will have to be sifted through, to decide what fits your guidelines and what does not, and you will need to let people know, if, and why, their amendments have been ruled out.

Compositing

This can be done by post, or by having a meeting before the conference starts (see also p. 148). If your rules do not lay anything down, then choose whichever is the most practical for your group. If you can do it by post in advance, then it will be possible to distribute copies to delegates right at the beginning of the conference, so they have time to digest them; possibly you could post them out the week before the conference. If you have to wait until the day of the conference, you'll need foolproof copying or duplicating facilities to allow you to quickly run off copies of what has been agreed.

You may, however, decide not to try to composite at all. If there is going to be time to discuss every motion separately, it is more democratic to do so. Groups have agreed to send in motions on particular points, not on all the others that may be lumped in with them. However, taking every motion can also make for a difficult and time-wasting discussion, if there are several motions which are almost but not quite the same, and people won't want to have to choose between them. They can also end up voting for everything, even if different points contradict each other, simply because the different motions do not bring out clearly enough what the points at issue are.

Perhaps the most sensible idea is to put groups with motions on the same subject in touch, and ask them to try to work out a joint motion if they can. If it looks as though your timetable is going to be very tight, it will be worth putting some pressure on them to do so. In some organizations, people can be ruled out altogether if they don't agree a composite, but this is a very authoritarian attitude.

If a group then turns up without having made moves to composite the motions, you could say that the time allowed for debating the subject as a whole remains the same, and therefore each person is allowed fewer minutes to speak, and offer them another chance to get together.

As organizers, you must do a balancing act. It is important that the conference gets through everything it has to cover, but without steamrollering or squeezing out individuals. It will help to carry out the balancing act successfully if you take care about explaining, clearly and often, what the difficulties are and why you are doing things in a particular way. To some people this will sound as though you are just making excuses, and they will continue to press their point. Others will be unreasonable whatever you say, perhaps because they care so passionately about the particular issue that they feel that anyone who stands in their way is deliberately obstructing them. Most people, however, respond to having difficulties explained to them. They may even be able to suggest a way round them.

Timetable planning

This should be roughed out quite early on before you book accommodation and make administrative arrangements, to see how much time is needed for the business. It is important to think about how you are going to allocate the time overall, before you invite any outside speakers. It is frustrating for the delegates to have to listen to a speaker if they know time for the policy discussion is slipping away.

However, sorting out the **final** timetable can't be done until all the motions, and amendments, are with you, so that you know exactly what you are dealing with. The planning group will then have to work out whether items can be grouped together for discussion, and if so how.

■ Ellen's playscheme conference, for instance, might have three motions on funding, four on the payment of staff, and one each on liaison with beat policemen, provision of free meals and links with youth workers.

They could either start on motion 1, and work through to 10, perhaps taking them in the order they came in to the planning group, or they could put the three motions on funding together and vote on the three in turn after they have gone over the whole subject in detail. They could then do the same with the four on payment of staff, and then take the three motions on separate subjects individually. The time allocated to each discussion would depend on how many motions there were. They might start with a basic 'unit' of 20 minutes per motion. So the discussion on funding will be 3 × 20 minutes, that is, an hour; that on paying staff one hour and 20 minutes, and the other three 20 minutes each. For a 'composite' or joint motion, allow a longer time than for a motion standing on its own, but less than you would for the two or three motions if they were standing by themselves. So a joint motion made up of four different ones might be allowed 50 minutes, rather than the hour and 20 minutes that four motions on their own would be allocated.

If time is short, you will have to work instead on the basis of 'sessions' and fit debates into them, no matter how many motions there are. Thus the session between the start and the coffee-break could be for funding, and the one between the coffee-break and lunch for the payment of staff.

What if a subject overflows, and you have got to lunchtime and are still deep in a discussion on funding? The chair's role is to try to stop this happening, but sometimes it is unavoidable, or s/he is simply overruled by the rest of the delegates who feel the subject is very important.

If your group has formal 'standing orders' these may lay down what is to happen in such cases. If not, then the planning group needs to decide and recommend something to the conference at the beginning. Alternatives are:

- any business that is unfinished at the end of one session is carried over to an 'overflow' session at the end; and the conference goes on to the next subject at the time the programme states;
- the session overruns, you start the next one late, and try to claw back the time later by cutting down another session. If anything gets lost altogether, it could either simply be forgotten, or your national committee or executive committee, if you have one, could deal with it.

The drawback with the first alternative is that if you are just getting into an important discussion, it is a shame to break it off and start on something else. When you pick it up again later, you will not feel the same enthusiasm. However, the second method can mean important issues don't get discussed at all.

A third possibility, if all of you have enough stamina, is to extend the hours of the conference and insert extra sessions to give you time for all the business. Some groups regularly carry on until midnight, but not all of us can do this, or want to! It would certainly cause difficulties for those with childcare responsibilities, or those who came from far away. Also, once people know this is going to happen, business tends to expand to fill the time available.

Conference arrangements

On the actual day of the conference, the planning committee will probably have to begin by handing out papers, sorting out seating arrangements, and so on, unless you can find people to help out with this, or have paid staff. At least one member of the committee should be available from the start to explain the procedure being used, and the timetable you are following, and answer any questions. There will always be people who have not read their papers, however early you send them out, and there will always be queries you haven't thought of. The planning committee should be available to meet during the conference in order to sort out any difficulties that have arisen. Having discussed an item, they must then **recommend** it to the conference, who can agree or disagree. It is best, but may not always be possible, to put these administrative reports about how you will handle the issues on paper, so that people can take them in more easily. For a small conference, an alternative might be a blackboard or a large sheet of paper placed somewhere where everyone can see it.

Stewarding

As people come into the conference, they will usually mill around in a confused way as they look for someone to answer their queries. There will be some who have lost their conference papers, some who are looking for the toilet, and some who want to know what time the lunch break is and what the arrangements are. It will help if you have desks clearly marked 'Information' or 'Enquiries' where people who know enough to answer such queries are situated. You also need people who move around and stand by the doors to show people where to go and answer questions. These are called **stewards** and it's helpful if they wear badges or armbands to say so. They should be patient and well briefed, so that they actually have the answers to the questions people ask.

You can reduce the number of questions by putting up large notices explaining the system for lunch, giving the timetable, and so on. However, don't expect that everyone, or even most people, will read them!

Chairing

Who is taking the chair at the conference? It is a very important role and this is not the time for people to learn how to chair. It should be someone experienced and, if possible, also impartial. If there are several people available who fit that description, they could take the job in turns. This would have a lot of advantages, because chairing is an exhausting task.

The chair needs to know, preferably through having a briefing sheet with everything written down:

- what the arrangements are for the debates and discussions; in particular how long people are allowed to speak (usually there is a limit of about five minutes, or perhaps a little longer for those putting forward resolutions);
- what the organizers have said to people about any special points (for example, that an emergency item can or can't be squeezed in the agenda);
- where to get hold of the organizing committee if anything needs sorting out.

Chapter 4 explains the role of the chair at a smaller meeting, and a conference differs only in terms of the numbers you have to deal with. The essentials, as always, are to be fair and good-tempered. You need to be tough about not letting people exceed the time limit. Don't let people interrupt or heckle the speakers either. Although interruptions may do no harm to the individual who's on his/her feet, it may put off others who are wondering if they dare get up.

Look all round the hall when you check who have their hands up waiting to speak, and keep a note of those who are trying to get a word in. If you don't know their names, write a list like this: 'man in red jersey on left'; 'white-haired woman at back'; and so on, to identify them. Alternatively, you could ask people to queue up to speak. The National Pensioners' Convention, for example, has a microphone on each side of the hall and people line up to speak. This is fair and it stops anybody moaning about having been missed out, although potential speakers do require stamina.

Another possibility is to ask people to send up their names on pieces of paper. You can then call them in the order in which they reach you, or take people for and against the proposals in turn. However, there can be suspicions of unfairness with this method. People can't see who is asking to speak, and so they tend to think that you are picking your friends.

Having agreed, with the organizing committee reports at the beginning of the conference, the ground rules you're working on, try to stick to them even if people start appealing for changes. But there will be times when the mood of the conference suddenly changes, and one can often sense this.

■ Martha is chairing a meeting where an elderly woman makes an incredibly passionate and moving speech about peace, and the whole conference is listening with bated breath. She doesn't cut her off at the end of five minutes, though she passes her a note reminding her of the time.

If the chair has any doubt what the feeling of the meeting is, then the best thing is to put it to them, without making a fuss about it, making plain that you're not regarding it as a vote of confidence (see p. 57). Ask them to vote, quickly, on a specific point.

■ The debate on rate-capping at your local government conference is very interesting and large numbers are queueing up to speak, but you're due to start the next item soon. So Anindya, who's chairing, asks the next speaker to wait a moment, and says, 'Because of the interest shown, I suggest we allow this discussion to go on for another fifteen minutes. This will involve reducing the next debate by the same amount. Can those who agree with this put up their hands. Those against.'

The danger with doing this is that someone may then propose a longer time, and someone else a shorter. Anindya will need to be careful not to let a wrangle develop. Since what people are really interested in is the subject you're discussing at the time, it is a good rule of thumb to keep discussion of any **secondary** subjects to the minimum. If they are unimportant anyway, eliminate them quickly with a vote. If they're important issues, but in the wrong place, suggest when the question can be discussed, and try to get the discussion back to the main subject as soon as you can.

Conference report

Give someone the responsibility of taking minutes or notes of the decisions if you are going to put together a report to go to your branches or your members afterwards. This is an important task and one that it is easy to forget if you are busy.

You could split this task up, if you have enough people. Writing notes takes concentration, especially if you want a report of what people said, and not just of what was decided. How full this note should be is another matter to be decided in advance.

Workshops

Is the conference going to stay as one meeting all the time? This is usually called a 'plenary' session. Conferences that are for discussion, rather than decisions, usually break into smaller groups, called 'workshops', for some sessions, and it is possible to do this even when the conference is there to take decisions, although it needs planning. For instance:

- If you are to be given reports by your executive members, you could split into smaller groups and ask each of those reporting to join a different group, and they could then move round the groups and give their reports several times.
- If there are several motions, or papers setting out a point of view, on the same subject, you could have a workshop in which they were put together into one motion or perhaps two opposing ones. This is an extension of the 'compositing' process explained on pp. 148–9. Having a discussion at the conference itself, when people have warmed up and are thinking about the subject, may be a better way of working out a joint motion than dealing with it by post or bringing people together before the conference starts.
- On complex issues, rather than requesting motions in advance, you could ask the people who are particularly interested to get together in a workshop – perhaps outside a normal conference session, for instance, during lunchtime or early evening if your timetable is very tight – and work out a motion then and there, to be presented to the rest.

  Remember, however, that a motion that has come up in this way has not gone through the same process as the others. Only the people at the conference have seen it and discussed it, and there has been no chance for the members to tell their delegates what they think. It has come out of the heads of people who are there, who are perhaps not very representative of the organization as a whole. Therefore an important policy should not be decided once and for all in this way. But the method can be useful to start the ball rolling, by putting together a proposal that can be discussed in the branches over the coming months.

■ Maeve's Labour Party groups want to start thinking about their policy on council house sales before the next election, 18 months away. So in a workshop at their conference, they put together the outlines of a policy, which they then circulate to the branches for them to discuss over the next year. At the following conference, it's the main item to be decided on.

- Even when the rest of the conference is about taking decisions, there may be some issues on which you want to pass on information, or give people a chance to learn skills, and these could be dealt with in smaller workshop groups.

■ With the abolition of the GLC, everyone at the London Resource Centres conference wants to learn about putting grant applications to charities. So the conference breaks into half a dozen small workshops, where people who have succeeded in getting grants explain the procedure to the others, and take them through the various stages on the application.

The benefit of going into smaller groups is that one can be less formal and people are less frightened about speaking. However, a lot depends on how small this group will be. If your conference is 180 strong, then breaking it into three groups of 60 will help a little, but people who are frightened by the idea of speaking to the whole conference will not find the idea of speaking to 60 people much less daunting, and you will still need a chair and a fair amount of self-discipline for the group discussion to be much use.

For a workshop group comprising more than half a dozen people you are likely to need a chair. You can ask for a volunteer to do this, at the beginning of the session, but it is usually easier if the planning committee asks someone in advance. There probably will not be enough time available to waste part of it while the members sit on their hands and hope someone else will volunteer. So most of them will be relieved if the job has already been allocated. The person taking the chair should be told what the arrangements are, and what is expected of him/her. It is a good idea to have a meeting of chairs in advance to brief them, even if this only takes place half an hour or so before the conference opens.

Do you require a record of what is said in each workshop? This could be either for the conference report afterwards, or for a verbal report to the full meeting (see the next section). Again, arrange someone in advance, if possible, and brief him/her on what is expected. If you cannot organize this, the chair should be asked to make this the first item s/he deals with, and should explain to the 'volunteer' (more likely someone press-ganged into it) what is needed.

Reporting back

This means that when you come back together as a full conference one person from each small group or workshop tells the conference what you have discussed and what conclusions you have reached. It is, unfortunately, a process full of pitfalls. Here are some of them:

- There are too many people to report back for the time available, especially if one or two people go on talking a long time.
- The workshops have been discussing the same thing, so that the reports are repetitive and therefore boring.
- People reporting back have not been given time to collect their thoughts, so that the reports ramble and the important points do not emerge clearly.
- No one was asked to report back in one particular group, so that there is an embarrassed silence when their turn comes.

How can you avoid these problems? First, think about whether a report back is necessary. If it was a session learning a skill, or passing on information about a particular item, you may be able to assume that those interested in that item went along to that session and there is no need for a further report to the rest. If the skills were practical ones, the 'report' could take the form of exhibiting what skills you have learnt. So, the people who have learnt about making a video could show it to the rest of the conference, or people who have worked on drafting leaflets could circulate copies of them.

Factual information can be written down and either displayed on a notice board or circulated at the time and again later with the conference report. People would take in more that way than if they have to absorb something in a highly condensed report.

If your workshops have been drawing up motions, then their 'report' would take the form of putting forward the motions. Give the person doing this on behalf of the group a time limit.

The chair should see that speakers come from outside the group that has been discussing the subject, as well as inside it. Since the group will all have been interested in the subject already, and will have gone deep into it during the workshop, there is a danger that they will hog the debate. Other people should have the opportunity to contribute, perhaps even to pour cold water if the group has been too enthusiastic or unrealistic. Keep the debate fairly short; the issue has already been thrashed out among those who are really involved, and this method is supposed to save time, rather than using up more.

When you need an ordinary report back, it is likely to work out better if:

- you givc each reporter a clear time limit, say, five minutes, and tell them in advance what it is;
- give them time to collect their thoughts in between the end of the workshop and the full session;
- explain **before** they start taking notes of the workshop what it is that you want. If you have a briefing session in advance, as suggested on p. 176, you could do this then; otherwise, get the person chairing each session to explain, or write down what you want and hand a sheet to each person volunteering to report back before they start actually doing so. Tell them, for instance, whether you want details of decisions only, or of the various views expressed, and whether you want to know what **action** people proposed. Work out what the purpose of the report back really is, and pass this information on. If you decide there really isn't a purpose, then perhaps you should decide not to have a report back after all, which will give you more time for discussion.

You might wish to have a written report to circulate afterwards, either as well as, or instead of, the verbal one. You will then need to ask people to hand over their notes to the organizers. Try to get them to do this at the end of the session, or as soon as they have written them out tidily. It will be much more difficult to get copies from them if they go away, even if they have promised you faithfully they will post the papers to you.

You might also want to hand out a questionnaire to conference participants, asking them what they thought of the conference and the particular workshops, how useful they were, and whether they should be repeated in future years. Include any interesting comments in your conference report, so that those who weren't there can see how things went. Here is an example of part of the report on a 'Women and Unemployment' conference held in 1984.

Women and Health
This was led by Pam Thorpe and Vera Mitchell from Brent Health Emergency Campaign. Once again, this was quite a small group which was good in that everyone was included in the discussion. Ways of running a successful 'Women and Health' course using the resources of unemployed centres was discussed. Personal canvassing for the course is better than leafleting; children's health issues were found to be a big draw and the course can then build up to the idea of women looking after their own health rather than just caring for others. An example of a weight-loss group that turned into a women and health course was discussed. One delegate wrote, 'I was disappointed, though not in the least surprised, that the women who led the workshop knew of no surveys that had investigated the effects of unemployment on women. I know of various studies relating to men and unemployment and had hoped to find out about work that is being done on women.'

Voting

Even if as individual branches you try to avoid taking votes, you will usually not be able to do so at a big conference; there will simply not be time to go on discussing until a consensus is reached. Usually, people would put up their hands to vote, but sometimes you may want a secret ballot or a recorded vote for particular issues; see pp. 156–7 for details of how these are conducted. The chair will need helpers to count. Again, these jobs can be spread around, with different people taking them on for particular sessions. You could ask for volunteers at the beginning, but it's more likely that you'll have to press-gang people into helping out. Spreading the job out has the advantage that people are less likely to accuse you of fiddling it than if all the counting is done by one small group.

Elections

At most conferences, you will be voting for the election of a committee. Not every organization does this; some groups leave everything to a particular branch for the year, but sooner or later a national body tends to emerge, if only to plan the next conference. The committee has first to be nominated and then voted upon. Nominating is the process of putting forward the names of people others want to see elected. It can either happen beforehand, or at the conference itself. If it's happening beforehand, you need to inform people in advance; tell them where to send the names; let them know what other information is required. For instance, do you need to have biographical details, and must they sign a form agreeing to the nomination? If so, when must this be done by?

If nominations are going to be taken on the day, from the conference itself, people will need to know in advance, so that they can come prepared. One additional point you should establish in this case is what happens if someone is nominated in his/her absence. How do you know if s/he is willing to stand? For unpopular jobs, like treasurer, it's quite a common event to 'volunteer' a person who isn't there. It is sometimes necessary to be strict about this and say that only people present, or those who have sent in a written letter of agreement, can be nominated. This may sound bureaucratic but it avoids the embarrassing and awkward situation where a committee starts its life with half a dozen gaps in it because the people put forward turned out not to be interested.

Having got the list of names together, do you want the candidates to speak and be prepared to answer questions? This method has disadvantages. It may mean that some people feel it is impossible for them to stand for election, because they have not got the nerve to talk in front of a large group. It could be particularly discouraging for women, and people from ethnic minorities. It can also mean that the most fluent person, rather than the most capable, wins. Moreover, it is a rather lengthy process and you may not feel that there is enough time for it at your conference.

An alternative is to get people to circulate written statements, though this can cause problems with the amount of paperwork you will have to produce. Try to arrange for the list of candidates to be read out, and each one to stand up so that people can see them, at some point in the conference. Putting names to faces will make it much easier for people to know who they are voting for, or against.

An explanation of the ways in which an election is usually organized at a conference is given on pp. 159–60. There is no way of avoiding a certain amount of bureaucracy on this, if you want your election to be seen to be fair. If it is generally considered chaotic, or to favour one group over another, the committee will not be regarded as 'legitimate', that is, as having the right to represent anyone else.

Winding up and following up

The organizing committee needs to decide in advance – and report to the conference at the beginning – about what happens to items that don't get covered. They could be dropped altogether; voted on quickly without discussion; or left to the permanent committee that runs your affairs in between conferences.

If your organization is without a permanent committee, or has one to whom you don't like to give too much power, then you will probably want to vote on everything quickly. However, if you have a suitable permanent committee, leaving it to them allows the subject to be discussed in depth, although by a smaller group.

What will happen to the decisions that you have made? Two things still need to be done: they need putting into effect; and the members need informing of what they were. Putting the decision into effect could mean several different things, depending on what each decision was.

- Tim's organization has decided to call a national demonstration in three months' time on racism in the media. The organizing committee should not let the conference end before a group to plan and organize this demonstration has been set up and people who are willing to help brought together to discuss it.

- Adrienne's group have decided to write to the Secretary of State expressing their anger at the cut in overseas aid. The permanent committee elected from the conference will be the ones to write the letter, and to follow up on the response.

Most follow-up work naturally falls on the new committee. If they don't have a fixed meeting date, then they need to decide when and where to meet next before dispersing from the conference, since this will avoid a lot of frantic phone calls trying to establish a date – any date – that more than two people can do. Most of the first committee meeting after the conference needs to be spent getting it clear what was decided and sorting out responsibility for putting it into effect.

Telling the members what happened sometimes involves producing a report word for word, as many trade-union conferences do. For most groups, however, this would be too big a task even to think about. It is more realistic to plan just to send out a list of resolutions passed, a report of the workshops, any factual information that had been promised, and perhaps a note of what any important guest speaker, or the leader of your organization, had said. This could go to each branch; each delegate who attended; appear as a report in your newsletter or magazine; or perhaps all of these.

Sending out the information is important, if the conference is going to be valuable not only to those who were there, but to the groups that sent them along. However, the planning committee may feel exhausted and flinch at the idea of yet more papers after the conference is finished. If so, get the new committee, rather than the old one, to do the donkey work of the post-conference mailing. The disadvantage of doing this is that it may lead to gaps and difficulties while the new people get themselves sorted out. The advantage, though, is that it is a good way of helping them learn their way round and of finding out the policies they are supposed to be putting into effect.

One way to reduce the cost, and the effort, of mailing is to ask every delegate who wants to be sent a report to provide a stamped addressed envelope. To make this easier, get together a supply of stamps and envelopes, so that they merely have to buy them and write the address.

The reporting back process is another point that needs to be decided on **before** the conference. Otherwise there may be a hiatus during which things are sorted out, and people's memories will fade and their notes will be lost, so that it will be much more difficult to establish what went on.

9.

Discussion conferences

A conventional discussion conference will usually be run simply as a series of lectures, with each speaker talking perhaps for half an hour or 40 minutes, then answering questions for a few minutes; after that the next person speaks. If the numbers are large, you may have a choice of parallel lectures. Otherwise, you remain in the same large groups all the time and there is very little chance to participate.

There is not much 'procedure' involved here. Each session has a chair who is responsible for seeing that people who want to ask questions are called in the right order and that no one monopolizes the floor. Often the delegates are so passive, in fact, that the chair finds s/he has to start the discussion off by asking the first question anyway.

Alternatives

Groups on the left are very fond of discussion conferences and adopt a procedure that started off as an alternative to the conventional one, but is now equally predictable and requires very little more real participation.

The format adopted is for the conference to have perhaps one or two 'plenaries', meetings of all the members in a single group, and then a series of smaller 'workshops' – meetings on different subjects conducted simultaneously. Often these are organized in 'streams', that is, all the workshops on, for instance, housing, would follow each other in one room, while in the next room people interested in social security would have their workshops at the same time. Some people remain in the same stream all the time, while others shop around.

The formula for the plenaries and the workshops is often the same; one or two people read out a prepared paper, taking up half the time that's been allocated or sometimes more, and the audience then have the rest of the time to ask questions or perhaps have some discussion. It's a formula that has been taken over from the university teaching style of lectures and seminars. It only works there because people are so used to it they don't question it, and there is really no reason why it should work particularly well in any other context.

The problems with this arrangement are:

- it allows for very little participation by the majority; the speakers are the stars, the rest are the passive audience;
- unless you take pages of notes – and there are plenty of people who do, but it's hard work – you don't actually take in much; it's extremely hard to concentrate on one person's voice for very long.

Some organizers, for instance, the Communist Party with its Great Moving Left Show in 1984, have tried to liven the proceedings up by introducing entertainments, cabaret, videos, and so on. All these ideas help – and you can get your political message across as well, or better, in many cabarets and videos than in a lecture – but they tend to be simply in addition to all the workshops and lectures.

The big plenaries probably can't be changed. It may be better to scrap them altogether, unless you have a real 'star' speaker whom everyone wants to hear, the leader of a political party or of a major protest group, for instance. Otherwise, stick to the workshop arrangement, but try to change the method.

The suggestions for dealing with visiting speakers given on pp. 93–5 can be adapted for use in larger conferences. Depending on the resources you've got, here are some possibilities:

- Ask people to get their papers ready in advance and send them out, or hand them out on the day, to those who register. This way the speaker can assume people have read these, and just run over the main points at the beginning, then invite people to ask questions, make suggestions, or criticize the paper. Duplicating or copying all the papers is expensive, but people are often willing to pay quite a lot for these conferences, so they may well be willing to stump up. Try to find a cheap source of copying or printing.
- If your budget won't run to this, or if your speakers are not organized enough to write their papers in advance, then at least you could circulate a one- or two-page summary, so that people have something to take away with them afterwards.
- Put together a short list of questions that the speaker is raising. This could be as well as, or instead of, the summary. It will help the discussion focus on particular aspects. A discussion paper for a session on housing, for instance, might say: What do you think should be the policy on council house sales? Will it be politically possible for Labour to say it will stop them? Should councils be building for sale?

- If the speaker is going to use excerpts from books, letters or other people's speeches in what s/he says, then it makes it more interesting if s/he hands them out to other members of the group to read. Simply having a change in the voice makes a difference to those listening, and the person actually reading will remember that piece, if no other.
- Try to present as much visual material as you can; photographs, posters, blow-ups of leaflets. You could either pass these round, or put them up on the wall and suggest people look at them as they come into the room.

It is important to have a chair for any workshop; don't expect the speaker to do it all. It's also wise to brief the people concerned about what's expected from them, especially if you are doing things in a different way from usual. They may well not have come across the ideas before and will need to have them explained. Either try to get people together in a meeting or else send them a clear, detailed letter setting out the main points. Follow it up with a phone call if you can. As with every type of meeting, the more prepared you are, the better it will be.

Afterwards

As with a decision conference, people will get more value out of it if you can circulate a report (see p. 179). It will be especially useful if you've been experimenting with methods to send out a questionnaire to see how the different ideas went down with people.

Checklist

This is intended as a quick reference sheet for the people responsible for putting together the procedure, the papers and the agenda. There is a similar checklist in *Organising Things* (see Further Reading, p. 210) for the nuts and bolts, like arranging food and sleeping accommodation, so it may be helpful to refer to that as well. This list applies to both decision and discussion conferences, although some items will not be relevant if, for example, you have no resolutions coming up. Check it through just the same, in case there's anything you've forgotten.

Planning the timetable

	Covered on page
What date is the conference?	165
When does the final mailing need to go out?	168
How long will it take you to get it ready?	166
Are you having:	
motions?	166
amendments?	166
compositing?	169
How long do you need to allow for:	
the motions to come in?	166–9
the amendments?	166–9
putting together the final agenda?	166–9
When does the first mailing have to go out?	167
What are the deadlines to include in that mailing?	168
When are the organizing group meeting to discuss the motions?	170
Have you roughed out the timetable for each day of the conference?	171
Have you issued invitations to speakers or special guests?	

Details

How many sets of papers are you going to have to send out?	165–70
How many pages?	165–70
Where are you getting them printed/copied/duplicated?	165–70
How much is postage going to cost?	165–70
Can you afford it?	165–70
Can any group provide their own copies?	165–70
Are there volunteers to do the collating and packing?	165–70

First mailing Covered on page

Who is it going to? — 167–8
Do you have all the addresses? — 167–8
Does it include details of:
when and where the conference is? — 167–8
what the arrangements are? (See the *Organising Things* checklist.) — 167–8
how people are to be nominated or elected? — 167–8
what the timetable is in the run-up to the conference? — 167–8
deadline dates? — 167–8
guidelines for motions? — 167–8
Are you also putting details in your newsletter or magazine? — 167–8

When replies come in

Who is looking after:
registering the delegates? — 168–9
deciding on which motions are in order? — 168–9
notifying the groups concerned? — 168–9
telling them how to challenge your ruling? — 168–9

Second mailing

Have you:
sent out the list of motions? — 169
given a deadline for amendments? — 169
given guidelines for amendments? — 169
included the timetable again? — 169
put more information in your newsletter or magazine? — 169
Have you:
decided which amendments are in order? — 169
told the groups concerned? — 169
told them how to challenge your ruling? — 169

Compositing

What arrangements have you made? Is it:
by post? — 169–70
by a meeting before the conference? — 169–70
at the conference? — 169–70

Covered on page

How are you hoping to make copies of the composited motions so that all involved can see them? ______ 169–70
How will you circulate these? ______ 169–70

Timetable

When are you meeting to finalize this? ______ 170–72
How are you grouping the subjects? ______ 170–72
Which ones will take a long time and which less? ______ 170–72
How much time are you allocating for each motion/composite/debate? ______ 170–72
What are you going to do if a subject overflows? ______ 170–72

At the conference

Who is handing out papers and answering queries? ______ 172–3
Is the organizing committee available to sort out problems? ______ 172–3
Who is doing the stewarding? ______ 172–3
When is the organizing committee reporting? ______ 173–4
Who is taking the chair? ______ 173–4
  Are you taking this in turns? ______ 173–4
Is there a briefing sheet for the chair? ______ 173–4
How long are speakers allowed to talk? ______ 173–4
What are the arrangements for calling people? Do they:
  put up their hands? ______ 174
  queue at the microphone? ______ 174
  send up notes? ______ 174
Are you having workshops? ______ 175–9
  What are they intended to achieve? ______ 175–9
  What are they going to do? ______ 175–9
  Who is chairing them? ______ 175–9
  Who is reporting back? ______ 175–9
  When? ______ 175–9
Have you allowed enough time for the reports? ______ 175–9
Are you issuing a written report of the conference? ______ 178
Who is collecting the notes from the workshops? ______ 178
Are you doing a questionnaire? ______ 179
Can you arrange to copy material so it can be circulated? ______ 179
Have you given the reporters:
  a briefing on what's expected of them? ______ 178
  a clear time limit? ______ 178
  time to collect their thoughts? ______ 178

Voting and elections	Covered on page
What procedure are you going to use?	179–80
Who's responsible for counting?	179–80
When do nominations have to be in?	179–80
Have all the candidates sent in biographies/statements?	179–80
Are they being asked to speak?	179–80
Do they know this?	179–80
What happens if a candidate isn't there?	179–80
What if there are fewer nominations than places?	179–80
When are you announcing the results?	179–80

Afterwards

What happens to items that are not discussed?	180–82
How are the decisions going to be put into effect?	180–82
How are you telling the members about it?	180–82
Who is carrying out the decisions?	180–82
Have you fixed a date for the next committee meeting?	180–82
Who is assembling the conference report?	180–82
When is it being sent out?	180–82
To whom is it being sent?	180–82

10.

The Law

Most people, most of the time, do not need to be involved with the law. Even if things go wrong in a group you're concerned with, it will usually be possible to sort it out without involving the courts or the police. There are times, however, when the courts could be involved, or you might want to use the law yourself.

There is no one Act of Parliament, or code of law, about meetings. There are different Acts that are relevant, and there is also what is called 'case law', that is, the framework that judges have created by the decisions that they have made over the years. This means that the legal position is not always clear, and there is often room for doubt. I have tried to say where the grey areas are, as I go through. Much depends on what sort of organization you are and the sort of meeting you are concerned with.

Statements about what the law says are sometimes used to make people take a particular course of action, or to frighten them off something. If you think that this is happening to you, check the real position. If necessary, get legal advice from a solicitors' firm, law centre or Citizens' Advice Bureau. Even if you have to pay for advice – it will be worth it in the long run.

If the courts are brought in, it's not only the findings in the case that matter. There may also be heavy legal costs. Even if you win, you may find yourself having to pay. This could happen for several reasons.

- if the people against you are legally aided, the judge will probably not make them pay your costs;
- if they are asked to, what they pay may not cover everything you've spent;
- if the judge decides the group 'brought it on themselves' by being careless, then even if you win the case he could make 'no order for costs', which means each side pay their own.

Acting outside your powers

The judges have built up a body of practice from previous cases, which they follow; this is called 'case law'. Trade unions, limited companies and local government bodies all have special kinds of law applying to them.

There are two main ideas behind judges' rulings on an organization's powers. The first of these is 'natural justice'; that is, a person must be seen to be treated fairly. In particular, people who have a particular interest or are likely to be biased should not judge another individual's case; and an individual who is likely to be penalized has a right to be given a warning that the issue is coming up and a chance to put his/her side of the case. So, for instance, when a few years ago the national executive of the Labour Party decided to expel six members of Militant, they had to invite them to come to a meeting to defend themselves, and then to put their case to the whole Labour Party Annual Conference.

The second issue is what is known legally as *ultra vires*. This means 'beyond your powers'. An organization with a written constitution will have a clause at the beginning setting out its aims and objectives.

However important the issue you want to deal with is, if it is not covered by these aims you do not have the powers to take it on. Many organizations take care, therefore, to make their aims and objectives as wide as possible to make sure they are not restricted. If the organization is also a charity, this clause has to be approved by the Charity Commissioners as well, and this means, broadly, that the objectives have to be linked either to 'the relief of poverty' or to 'education'. So, for example, the Resource Project constitution says, in legal language:

> The objects for which the Project is established are, for the benefit of the community, to provide legal advice, assistance and representation with a view to
>
> (1) the relief of poverty, suffering and distress among persons resident or working in the Borough; and
>
> (2) the advancement of education of persons resident or working in the London Borough of——.

Their next clause is headed 'Powers' and says that 'in furtherance of the aforesaid objectives but not otherwise the Project may do all things necessary or expedient'.

This means that, if challenged in the courts, the Project would have to prove that it was acting 'in furtherance' of its objectives; if it could not show this then it would be acting *ultra vires*. So running a stall at a local festival with copies of their literature would be covered; taking part in a festival in Paris probably would not be. If a group decides to do something that the court considers is outside their powers, the decision is invalid for the group. If any money has been spent, it becomes the personal responsibility of the people concerned, which would usually mean the management committee members who voted for it.

Breach of procedure

Another area in which the law is occasionally brought in is the procedure at meetings. Cases on this are not common; the judges usually do their best to leave such questions to the group itself to sort out. Reluctantly, they will intervene where the meeting is considering 'matters of general public concern' or administering something that is of local interest or belongs to all the members of the organization. So a judge would not be interested in the way your group organized a summer picnic; but if you owned a building, and had decided to sell it to the highest bidder, they would say the case was a suitable one for them, and would want to check that the decision had been properly made.

They would look first at the rules of the organization. Was the meeting at which the decision was taken conducted in line with those rules? If, for instance, the rules said that at least six people including the chair and secretary had to be there, they would check this point.

On questions which the rules did not cover, they would follow the common law. This is not written down in one place, it is the accumulation of decisions made over many years in other court cases. Sometimes a judge will quote a nineteenth- or even eighteenth-century court case as justification for his views. The judges have tended to regard the standard procedure for formal meetings, copied from Parliament and codified by Citrine and Hannington (see p. 37), as being 'correct'. They will consider that if you have followed the procedure – which is explained in Chapters 1–5 of this book – you have made your decision in the right way. They have not been asked to decide on cases where a meeting has been run in the informal, unstructured manner common in the peace movement or the women's movement. A meeting that was completely informal would probably be beyond their understanding, and they would say it was not a real meeting at all. At the least they would look for:

- a person in the chair;
- evidence that people had been properly notified;
- a record of how many people were at the meeting;
- a record of what decisions were taken, and evidence of how they were reached; was a formal resolution put, did people know what they were voting on, did they have a chance to discuss and amend it?

A meeting could certainly be run in an informal way, without being authoritarian or threatening, and still include all this. This book suggests that you should anyway keep all these points in mind as guidelines. However, many groups would not have done everything in this list. For instance, often only the people who are at one meeting get to know when the next one is, because no formal notice is sent out. If someone were to challenge a decision taken at one of these meetings, you could be in trouble. It's therefore sensible to make sure, if you're dealing with a large sum of money, or with something that a lot of people feel very strongly about, or with anyone you're employing, that you do keep to these basic guidelines, which are good practice anyway.

If a court case was threatened, the lawyers' first step would be to find out the precise legal status of the organization. This was explained in Chapter 1, so you may need to refer back to that. The legal system depends on having someone to take action against. This can be an individual, or something like a company or a trust which has a 'legal personality', which means that the law regards it as being a person.

Voluntary organizations, such as residents' groups, have not usually been set up formally enough to have a legal personality, so they are 'unincorporated associations'. The judges regard these as simply collections of individuals. So, in the case of the Utopia Residents' Association it is not the committee as a body that Jane and Fred are suing; it is Bill, Peter, Ashraf, Mary, Moira, the rest of the committee. If the case goes against these people, they would then have to pay any costs out of their own pockets, not out of the Association's funds. In many cases they could insure themselves; if they hadn't done so they might regret it.

If your organization is a company, however, it is usually the company, as a legal entity, that is sued; though the courts might still say that individuals had to pay up instead, if they had acted unwisely.

Problem cases

The way in which the law could get involved is best shown by an example.

■ Utopia Residents' Association own a minibus and a set of video equipment. At their July meeting, the committee decide to sell both and buy a shetland pony so that they can give the children rides. Various people are unhappy about the decision.

Jane Phillips is one of the committee members. She goes to a solicitor who starts a case in the High Court against the rest of the committee for an injunction. This is a legal ruling to stop something happening; in this case, to stop the sale going ahead. Her 'grounds', that is, her reasons for doing this, might be that although she is a member of the committee, she was not told the meeting was taking place, and that too few people were at the meeting for it to have been properly constituted.

Injunctions are for emergencies; Jane has to act fast in this case to stop the van and video being sold. The court listens to her side of the case, and decides whether 'prima facie', which means on the face of it, that is, after looking quickly at it, Jane has good reasons for stopping the sale. The court also looks at what is called the 'balance of convenience', that is, whether stopping the sale will cause more problems than letting it go ahead and decides that it would not, and so grants an injunction, which is delivered to the people who were going to sell the van and video. At this stage it is usual also to ask the plaintiff to give an 'undertaking in damages'. This means that if, when the case comes to court for a full hearing, Jane loses, she may have to compensate the other side for any financial loss they might have had because of the case.

If the others ignore the injunction, they are in contempt of court and could be fined or imprisoned. A few months later a full court case will be heard, where both sides would put their views about the issue as a whole.

In another case, Fred Ormerod, an ordinary member of a tenants' association, is angry about a disco being held, because he considers it a misuse of his money. He therefore decides to sue the committee for acting outside their powers (*ultra vires*). He also gets a solicitor, who goes to the High Court and sues the committee members. He wants a declaration from the court that the committee were wrong, and a judgement that if any money has been spent as a result of the wrong decision, the committee are personally liable. In that case, if one of the committee had voted against the decision to run the disco, made it clear why, and disassociated himself/herself from it, that person would probably not be liable; but the rest would. If, like Jane Phillips, you could prove that you had never been informed about the meeting anyway, you would be safe.

Other areas of the law

This section contains a brief outline of some of the other areas of the law you may come up against. Hiring a room is covered in more detail in Chapter 8 of *Organising Things* (see Further Reading, p. 210), and the law on libel and slander in Chapter 3, so look at those if necessary.

Hiring a room

The owner of a hall can refuse to let you hire it, without giving a reason, so long as s/he is not discriminating on grounds of race or sex. Local authorities have to allow any candidate to hold a public meeting in a school during an election campaign for Parliament or the local council.

If the owners of a hall have agreed to let a room out and then change their minds, look at the small print in the contract you have signed. If it is written in that they reserve the right to do this, you will have no comeback. If there is no clause saying this, you may have the right to take them to court in a civil case, for an injunction and for damages. The threat may be enough, or you could try whipping up local publicity and pressure, for instance, a letter-writing campaign.

In legal terms a person who lets a room to you is 'licensing' you to use it, on certain conditions. If you break the conditions, you lose the licence and can be asked to leave. You may be regarded as trespassing if you don't go. The owner could have you removed, or call in the police to clear the room. If you're caught overcrowding, you may be asked to leave. You can offer to reduce the number of people in the room, but legally that doesn't change the fact that you have already broken your licence.

Refusing admission

The organizers of a meeting have the right to refuse admission, without giving a reason, whether there is an entry fee or not. If people force their way in, they are trespassing; the organizers are entitled to throw them out, using 'reasonable force' under the Public Order Act 1936.

Once people have paid an entry fee, they can be lawfully removed only if they disrupt the meeting and then refuse to leave when asked to do so. If you don't charge, they can be ejected at any time, without warning. If they are actually trying to break up the meeting, the Public Meeting Act 1908 entitles you to remove them, and you can ask for police help in doing so. However, before doing this you might try asking him/her quietly to go away, explaining your reason. If this doesn't work, once the meeting starts, explain to everybody what the problem is, and ask them to vote whether to allow the person to stay or not. If there is general agreement that s/he should go, get a couple of people to escort him/her out, and then ensure that there are people on each door to stop him/her coming back.

Alternatively, if the person is refusing to leave and you don't want a scene, or don't think you can carry it through, freeze him/her out; ignore any remarks s/he makes and pretend s/he simply doesn't exist.

You have to be very thick-skinned to withstand this for long. In the last resort, you might have to close the meeting.

Police have no right to come unasked to meetings held on private premises, unless they reasonably believe that a breach of the peace is likely to be committed (see next section). So if a uniformed bobby turns up at your peaceful group meeting, you have the right to ask him/her to go. Plain-clothes police often turn up at political meetings without authorization, and prosecutions are sometimes brought based on their evidence of what was said there. If you think someone is a plain-clothes police officer, try challenging him/her publicly; even if they deny it and stay, it will make people more careful about what they say.

Disorder

The Public Meeting Act 1908 makes it an offence to break up meetings, or to take them over, or forcibly replace the person in the chair. The Act isn't often used; usually people will have committed a more common offence, like breach of the peace, as well, and will be charged with that instead.

If there is trouble at a meeting people would probably be charged with insulting, threatening, or abusive behaviour likely to cause a breach of the peace.

Insulting words and behaviour are offences if a person at any public meeting:

- uses threatening, abusive, or insulting words or behaviour;
- distributes or displays any 'writing, signs, or visible representation' which is threatening, abusive, or insulting, through which a breach of the peace may be caused. This would include a leaflet or a placard.

'Threatening', the NCCL say, is defined as 'any behaviour which causes people of ordinary firmness or maturity to fear physical harm to themselves or their property'.

'Abusive' is vaguer, but generally means some verbal hostility which is likely to provoke disorder. The words you use, or your behaviour, need not be abusive to everyone, but to a particular group in your audience. In 1963 there was a court case in which a group of fascists had insulted Jewish people at a public meeting. The judge said that even if the speaker had not expected Jews to be present, he must 'take the audience as he found them' and he was therefore found guilty.

A 'breach of the peace' means that someone intentionally uses, or threatens to use, violence against someone else. To be charged with this, all you need to be doing is acting in a way that means a police officer can have a reasonable suspicion that you, or someone else because of you, might cause a breach of the peace. A judge said in 1960, 'There must exist proved facts from which a constable could reasonably have anticipated such a breach . . . it is not enough that he believes that there was a remote possibility, but there must be a real possibility of a breach of the peace.'

Once the police have arrived at the meeting, and started arresting people, you could be accused of obstruction if you did anything to stop them doing their job. This would include, for example, barring their entry to a meeting, or refusing to close it when they had ordered you to do so.

If a meeting becomes really violent, you could find yourself charged with offences such as unlawful assembly and riots. An 'unlawful assembly' exists when three or more people get together to commit a crime, or to do something, whether legal or not, in a way which 'endangers public peace', or makes reasonably sensible people afraid that there is going to be a breach of the peace.

A 'riot' is defined as a 'tumultuous disturbance' by three or more people who have come together to carry out a common purpose, and to help each other, by force if necessary, against people who oppose them. They need to use enough force and violence to alarm reasonable people. In recent cases, this has been stretched to mean you are guilty even if you did not know the assembly was likely to be 'riotous'. It can carry heavy penalties.

A person involved in a fight could also be charged with 'affray', which means a fight in the presence of other people, some of whom become afraid. You can be charged with this if you were encouraging the fight with your presence. The prosecution would have to show that this was what you intended, that is, that you were deliberately egging people on.

If there is serious disruption at a meeting, then, like it or not, you will probably have to call the police; a member of the audience may well do so if you don't. However, before it reaches that stage the person running the meeting is going to have to take the crucial decision whether to abandon it, or to struggle on. It may well look worse from the platform than from the floor. If there seems no hope of the speakers making themselves heard, ask them what they want to do and, if they agree to give up, comply.

If you do have stewards, ask them to surround the disruptive group, but don't let them start a fight. If it looks as if they can escort them out peacefully, request them to do so. Much will depend on who is actually doing the disrupting; if it is the National Front, everyone else is likely to want them thrown out; if it is a group of anarchists, a number of people may sympathize with them and you will have to be more tactful.

Defamation

This can be a serious problem with things said at meetings or subsequently published. The word 'defamation' covers both slander and libel. Libel is in writing, slander is in speech. Thus you would **slander** another person at a meeting, but the secretary would then **libel** that person if the accusation was written into the minutes. This section mainly covers **slander**, as it is more likely to apply in the context of a meeting.

To prove that a person has been slandered, s/he usually has to prove that his/her reputation has been damaged. (For libel there need be no evidence about damage.) This means that something untruthful has been said publicly which tends:

- to lower him/her in the estimation of society;
- to make him/her hated, ridiculed or disliked by society;
- to make people feel contemptuous of him/her, or avoid his/her presence.

'Society' means conventional, 'right-thinking' people. There are four things that simply saying is slanderous, even if it has had no effect on the reputation of the person concerned:

- that someone has committed a criminal offence serious enough to be punishable by death or imprisonment;
- 'allegations of unchastity or adultery, if made against a woman' (yes, really);
- imputing that, at the time of the slander, the person had an infectious disease;
- alleging something calculated to disparage the person in their office, trade or profession at the time of saying it.

The person who claims to have been slandered is called the 'plaintiff'. S/he has to show that the speech referred to them, or could be taken as doing so. If you had actually been referring to someone else but had, say, used a nickname which could be taken to refer to that person, you could have unintentionally slandered them. So if you mention, for instance, 'Nobby Clarke of X Street', referring to a rotten landlord you have strong evidence against, you could find you have slandered another Nobby Clarke in X Street whose friends now thought he was a rotten landlord. If you make a general comment, it could be slanderous if:

- you mention someone's name in conjunction with it; if for instance you said, 'Only criminals go to the XYZ club. Mr P. was seen there last Wednesday'; or
- someone could deduce what you meant by the implications of what you said. This is called 'innuendo'. An example is, 'A person not a million miles away from Mr P. was seen handing over money to a policeman on Friday.'

If you slander an unnamed person who is one of a small identifiable group, then each person in the group could take you to court. So if you said the six members of a board of directors were stupid and dishonest, any or all of them could take action. You don't need to imply the person is at fault for it to be slanderous. So if you said someone had been mentally ill, it could be slanderous, even though it's not their fault.

You can defend yourself in five possible ways:

- demonstrating that what you said was true (not just that you believed it was);
- demonstrating that the words were 'fair comment' – that it was an opinion, not malicious, about a matter of public concern. This can't be used about a person's moral character;
- privilege. Some people, like MPs and judges, can say more or less what they like in Parliament or in the courts;
- qualified privilege. This covers people reporting fairly and accurately court cases and Parliament, provided there was no malice in their reports; and public meetings;
- innocent defamation. This is a very difficult defence to use. It means saying that you did not intend to be defamatory and took reasonable care to avoid making the mistake. You must make an offer of amends as soon as possible. This usually means publishing a correction and an apology in a newspaper or in the group's publication.

Before a case gets to court, you can state that the slander was made without malice or gross negligence, and offer to publish a full apology. You may also need to offer money. If the plaintiff accepts, the case would not then go to court.

Slander cases are not very common, but you do need to take care. You can avoid the straightforward slander by taking care over what you say, but if you are in any doubt, or if you have had a letter from someone threatening action, don't try to manage on your own. Get legal advice. Defamation is a specialized area of the law; find a local expert by asking the local newspaper who checks their stories. Phone up and ask to speak to the Editor, or the branch secretary of the NUJ, who is called the Father or Mother of the Chapel.

Official bodies

If you are a member of an official body, like a council, health authority, or board of school governors, there will be special rules governing your meetings. If there is any doubt about whether they are being run in line with these rules, ask at the meeting for legal advice to be taken from the relevant authority's solicitor, and for it to be made available to you. If it is a contentious issue, or you doubt what you are being told, you may have to get your own legal advice – which could be expensive, so try to do it as a group rather than just one person on his/her own.

Local government law in particular is now a very complex area, and certain lawyers specialize in it. The national headquarters of the Labour Party or a pressure group you are involved with ought to be able to find someone suitable, if the case is one in which they have an interest; otherwise, try contacts in other authorities to see if they have any useful experience, or phone the local government correspondent of one of the national newspapers or magazines.

Appendix 1.
'Meetingspeak'

This is a glossary of the words and phrases that the hacks, people who spend all their spare time at formal meetings, use. Check this list for what they mean. If you find yourself using any of them, beware – are you turning into a hack yourself?

With respect/with great respect/with very great respect

These all mean the opposite. How strongly they mean it depends on the tone that's used. Roughly, 'with respect' means you're wrong. 'With great respect' means you're utterly wrong and an idiot for thinking that, and 'with very great respect' means you're the most stupid person the speaker has ever come across and the ideas are absurd.

Through the chair

Doesn't mean you are kneeling down and peering through the bars of one. It means that you are responding to what someone else has said. As explained on p. 54, the formal rule is that you talk to the meeting as a whole, via the chairperson, not directly to that individual.

Move the vote be put

Shorthand for 'I propose that we vote on this item.' People go in for this sort of shorthand, dropping out words and phrases, a lot in meetings, perhaps because they feel they will get more done that way. They don't.

I will be brief

Means the opposite: 'I will go on and on.' A variation is, 'Briefly, as X has said what I was going to say . . .' This means, 'Not only will I go on and on, but I will also repeat what has been said already several times.'

Without wishing to be bureaucratic/obstructive/destructive

Means, 'I am now going to be bureaucratic/obstructive/destructive.'

Move standing orders are suspended for 10 minutes

Means, 'We're running out of time, so I propose we keep the meeting going for another 10 minutes and then stop' (see p. 58).

Order, order

This is what the chair says at the beginning of each meeting, or when people are talking among themselves, in order to stop the private conversations and get them to participate in the meeting. 'I call the meeting to order,' is a variation. They are both borrowed from Parliament and mean, 'Shut up and listen' (see p. 99).

Correct record

Not what you buy in a high street shop. It is usually used about the minutes, or notes of a previous meeting, and means that what went on there is accurately reported. 'Move the minutes are a correct record,' therefore means, 'Let us agree that the report is accurate' (see p. 101).

Thrown open to the meeting

Means that, once the people introducing an item, or those proposing or seconding a motion, have spoken, anyone else can speak. It's not a free-for-all, though; if you decide you want to speak you have to 'catch the chair's eye', by putting up your hand, waving your agenda paper around, or otherwise drawing attention to yourself.

Move nominations cease/close

Another bit of shorthand. When you are having an election (see p. 130) the chair will ask to begin with, 'Can I have nominations for X please?' People's names are put forward, and when it looks as if there are enough, or when people are bored, someone will say, 'Move nominations cease/close,' which means, 'Let us stop nominating people now, and get on with the election.'

Having the floor

The person who is talking at any one time 'has the floor'. The logic behind this bit of jargon escapes me; it just exists.

Giving way

If a person is speaking, and someone else wants to interrupt, the speaker **gives way** if s/he allows the interruption. In the House of Commons people ask, 'Will the member give way?', but people don't say this much elsewhere.

Giving notice

This means you announce something in advance. So you might **give notice** of a motion you are going to ask the meeting to discuss later.

Reserving the right

The person introducing the motion (see p. 40) can propose it 'formally', that is, without making a speech about it. S/he will then 'reserve the right to reply' to make clear s/he is not giving up the chance to make a speech altogether, but only at this stage. It's not really necessary to say this, as people would not assume you had given up your right, but it is a habit.

In order/out of order

Doesn't mean whether things are tidy or working properly. It refers to whether they're in line with various rules and procedures. If something is 'out of order' the chair can rule that it must not be discussed, or that the discussion must stop. The way you challenge these rulings is covered on pp. 55–6.

Making a ruling

What a chair does when s/he decides whether something is 'in order' or not (see above). If you disagree, you then 'challenge the ruling' (see pp. 55–6).

Reference back

If there's a report to your meeting, perhaps from a subcommittee or the executive committee, and you think the decision made is wrong and needs changing, you can 'move the reference back', which means they are told to reconsider. This happens all the time at Labour Party conferences (see pp. 150–51), usually to no effect.

Chairman

An old word for chair. Sometimes also described as 'Mr Chairman' or even 'Madam Chairman'. Some groups still use it and, for them, changing the name of the 'chairman' arouses considerable hostility. There are people who denounce it, at one and the same time, as utterly trivial and not worth bothering about, and a threat to civilization as we know it.

The most recent (1982) edition of Citrine (see p. 37) says pompously, 'For us, chairman is neuter and does not denote sex; you can have a male or female chairman.'

If pressed on why the name should not be changed, if it's so trivial and 'You're making a fuss about nothing,' such people usually mutter something about 'chairperson' being an ugly word, or 'not liking to talk to inanimate objects' if you suggest using the word chair. You may as well press the point. The argument is really more about attitudes and not about a word, so they will argue about something else if not that. If they really don't like 'chair', try 'president' instead.

Appendix 2.

A guide to etiquette

This is also not entirely serious. It is a list of the do's and don'ts for meetings – first the formal ones, then the informal ones, as many of their participants have an equally strong sense of what's right and what's wrong.

Formal meetings

Don't start knitting or sewing. It is not sufficiently serious for these terribly important meetings. It is also distracting for other people.

Do by all means:
read the *Guardian* (or the *Daily Mirror*);
read the papers for the next meeting you're going to – it shows how busy you are;
get out your diary and start flipping pages over, especially if you can demonstrate how busy you are;
empty and clean your pipe, fill it and then use up to a dozen matches to light it;
none of these is distracting for other people.

Don't take a toddler to the meeting;
say you can't get there because you won't be able to get a childminder;
arrive late at a meeting that starts at the children's teatime, or at 9.30 on a Saturday, with the feeble excuse that you've had to feed the kids or get the shopping.

Do announce that you can't come to the next meeting because your football club's playing away that night;
leave the room halfway through an important discussion to find out the cricket scores;
leave early to watch 'Match of the Day'.

Don't talk about your personal experience in a speech;
be emotional;
suggest that perhaps, maybe someone is on an ego trip or trying to make you feel guilty.

Do be pompous and repetitive;
find all sorts of high-sounding reasons for doing something you want to do anyway or that suits your interests;
always make it plain that you're not standing for election because you want the job, it's always because other people can't manage without you.

Informal meetings

Don't expect the meeting will start on time – it never does;
get impatient when it doesn't.

Do arrive 20 minutes late and sit around chatting until someone gets the nerve together to suggest you start, and that s/he will take the notes.

Don't try to hurry people into making a decision, even if it's getting late and you're all agreed. They'll accuse you of being authoritarian.

Do go round in circles discussing the same thing for hours and return to the question you thought you'd just finished 20 minutes ago. It makes things much more friendly.

Appendix 3.

Sample trust deed

This TRUST DEED is made the ______________________
day of ____
BETWEEN
____
____
hereinafter referred to as 'the Trustees' which expression shall where the context so permits include the Trustee or Trustees for the time being of this Deed.

WHEREAS
The Trustees are desirous of establishing a charitable trust as hereinafter provided and have provided the sum of ____________ (£________) to be held together with such other cash investments land or chattels as may from time to time be donated to or otherwise acquired by the Trustees upon with and subject to the trust's powers and provisions of this deed

NOW IT IS HEREBY AGREED AND DECLARED AS FOLLOWS:
1. The name of the Trust shall be 'Toucan Theatre Trust' (hereinafter referred to as 'the Trust').
2. The objects of the trust shall be by such means as are charitable and not otherwise:
   To advance education through drama music movement and mime and to encourage the development of community theatre in general.
3. The Trustees shall have to following powers in pursuance of the objects of the Trust and not otherwise:
(a) To promote present or arrange performances theatrical productions tutorials workshops exhibitions meetings and promotions of schemes of a charitable nature whether on any premises of the Trust or elsewhere.
(b) To open and maintain a bank account or bank accounts for the retention of the funds of the Trust and to make such regulations as they shall decide for the operation of such account or accounts.

(c) To raise funds by subscription donation appeal or otherwise for the purposes of the Trust.
(d) To invest monies belonging to the Trust and not required for immediate application for its objects upon such investments securities or property as they may think fit but so that monies subject or representing property that are subject to the jurisdiction of the Charity Commissioners for England and Wales shall only be invested in such securities as may for the time being be prescribed by law.
(e) Subject to such consents as may be required by law to borrow for the objects of the Trust such monies at such rates of interest and in such manner as they may think fit.
(f) To purchase take on lease or in exchange hire or otherwise acquire any real or personal property and any rights or privileges which the Trustees may think necessary for the promotion of the objects of the Trust and to construct maintain look after any buildings or erections necessary for the work of the Trust.
(g) Subject to such consents as may be required by law to sell let mortgage dispose of or turn to account all or any of the property or assets of the Trust as may be thought necessary with a view to the promotion of the objects of the Trust.
4. The Trustees shall out of the monies received by the Trust pay all proper expenses of administration and management of the Trust including the payment of any staff employed by the Trustees for the promotion of the objects of the Trust and shall use the residue of such monies as it thinks fit for or towards the objects of the Trust.
5. No Trustee shall be appointed to any salaried post of the Trust as hereinbefore provided or take or hold any interest in the Trust save in the capacity of Trustee or receive any remuneration or interest in the supply of goods or services at the cost of the Trust.
6. The Trustees shall not be bound in any case to act personally but shall be at full liberty to employ and pay any clerk or other agent or servant to transact all or any business of whatever nature required to be done in pursuance of the trusts herein including the day-to-day management of the Trust and the receipt and payment of all money and shall be entitled to be allowed and paid all charges expenses so incurred and shall not be responsible for the defaults of any such servant or agent or any loss occasioned by his or her employment.
7. The Trustees of this deed shall be no less than three and no more than seven.
8. The power of appointing new trustees hereof shall be vested in the surviving or continuing Trustees for the time being (excluding any retiring Trustee).
9. In the event of the winding up of the Trust the available funds of the Trust shall be transferred to such one or more charitable bodies

having objects similar or reasonably similar to those hereinbefore declared as may be chosen by the Trustees and approved by the Charity Commissioners for England and Wales.

10. The Trustees hereof for the time being shall be empowered to vary the terms and conditions of this trust by deed, provided that no amendment shall be made which would cause the trust to cease to be a charity in law.

IN WITNESS whereof the parties hereto have set their hands and seals the day and year first above written.

SIGNED SEALED AND DELIVERED by)
)
)
in the presence of)

SIGNED SEALED AND DELIVERED by)
)
)
in the presence of)

SIGNED SEALED AND DELIVERED by)
)
)
in the presence of)

SIGNED SEALED AND DELIVERED by)
)
)
in the presence of)

Further reading

Bloom and Norton, *Accounting and Financial Management for Charities*

Michael Cannell and Norman Citrine (eds), *Citrine's ABC of Chairmanship*, London: NCLC Publishing Society, 1982

S. Clarke, *Working on a Committee*, London: Community Projects Foundation, 1978

John Edgington and Susan Bates, *Legal Structures for Voluntary Organizations*, London: Bedford Square Press/National Council for Voluntary Organisations, 1984

Wal Hannington, *Mr Chairman*, London: Lawrence & Wishart, 1950

Trevor Lloyd and Andreas Michaelides, *How to Manage Your Money, If You Have Any: An Accountancy Handbook for Community Organisations*, London: Community Accountancy Project, 1983

Michael Locke, *How to Run Committees and Meetings*, London: Macmillan, 1980

Jeremy McMullen, *Rights at Work*, London: Pluto Press, 1983

Andrew Phillips, *Charitable Status: A Practical Handbook* (2nd edn), London: Interaction, 1982

Daniel Plesch (ed.), *What Do We Do After We've Shown the War Game?*, London: CND, 1982

Mark Smith, *Organise!*, Leicester: National Association of Youth Clubs Publications, 1981

Sue Ward, *Organising Things*, London: Pluto Press, 1984

Index

Acts of Parliament will be found grouped together under Acts of Parliament.